W. NEWMAN & CO.'S HAND-BOOK TO CALCUTTA

W. NEWMAN & CO.'S HAND-BOOK TO CALCUTTA

Historical And Descriptive, with a plan and Illustrations

KNIGHT JAMES BLACKBURN

GYAN

Published by

Gyan Publishing House
5, Ansari Road
Daryaganj, New Delhi-110002
Phone: 011-47034999, 9811692060
E-mail: books@gyanbooks.com

Distribution Network
gyanbooks.com
India, USA, Canada, UK, Australia

ISBN: 978-93-7097-689-4 (PB)

First Published, 1875

2nd Impression 2025

Printed at: Gyan Press, Delhi.

W. NEWMAN & CO.'S HAND-BOOK TO CALCUTTA
Author: KNIGHT JAMES BLACKBURN

Plan
of
CALCUTTA
Scale 1½ Inches = 1 Mile
Branch Post Offices
Pillar Post Offices
REFERENCES.
1 Free Church Institution.
2 Great National Theatre Hall (Native)
3 Bengal Theatre Hall (Native.)
5 Christ's Church.
6 General Assembly's Institution.
7 General Female School.
8 Leper Asylum.
10 K. C. Sen's Brahmo Somaj.
11 Mayo Native Hospital.
12 The Mint.
14 Roman Catholic Cathedral.
15 Greek Church.
16 Presidency College.
17 Hare School.
18 Calcutta University.
19 Eye Infirmary.
20 Hindoo College.
21 Police Hospital.
23 Commissary Depot.
24 Gas Works.
25 Bonded Ware-house.
26 Custom House.
27 General Post Office.
28 Writer's Buildings.
29 Police Office.
30 Town Guard.
31 Magistrate's Office.
32 Medical College Hospital.
34 Small Cause Court.
35 Metcalfe Hall.
36 Foreign Department.
37 St. John's Church.
38 Government Press.
39 Stationery Office.
40 Bengal Secretariat, P. W. Dept.
41 Bank of Bengal.
42 Reservoir Water Works.
43 New High Court.
44 Town Hall.
45 Legislative Department.
46 Government House.
47 Treasury.
48 Lord Bentinck's Statue.
49 Government Dispensary.
50 Telegraph Office.
51 Old Mission Church.
52 Dalhousie Institute.
53 Currency Office.
54 Baptist Chapel.
55 Military Department.
56 St. Xavier's R. C. Church.
57 Wellington Square.
58 Sealdah Small Cause Court.
59 Sealdah Magistrate's Cutcherry.
60 Campbell Medical School Hospital.
61 Union Chapel.
62 Corinthian Theatre.
63 Municipal Office.
64 Municipal Market.
65 Opera House.
66 Lord Lawrence's Statue.
67 Lord Harding's Statue.
68 Ochterlony Monument.
69 Theatre Royal.
70 Home Department.
71 Bengal Secretariat Office.
72 Imperial Museum.
73 United Service Club.
74 Asiatic Society.
75 Free School.
76 St. Thomas' Church.
77 Mahomedan College.
79 Free Church of Scotland.
80 European Female Asylum.
82 Police Hospital.
83 Boswell Hall.
84 School.
85 St. James' Church.
86 Baptist Mission Chapel.
87 Baptist Chapel.
88 Baptist Mission Press.
89 St. Thomas' R. C. Church.
90 Surveyor General's Office.
91 Doveton College.
93 Sir James Outram's Statue.
94 Bengal Club.
95 Commissariat Office.
99 St. Xavier's College.
100 Revenue Survey Office.
102 St. Thomas' Church.
103 St. Paul's Cathedral.
104 Bishop's Palace.
105 La Martiniere School.
106 Girl's Department.
107 House of Correction.
109 Government Telegraph Store Yard.
110 Insane Hospital.
111 Military Hospital.
113 Lunatic Asylum.
114 General Hospital.
115 London Mission Institute.
116 Body Guard Stables.
117 Government Dockyard.
118 P. and O. Company's House.
119 Kidderpore Church.
120 Upper Orphan School.
121 Lieut. Governor's House.
122 King of Oude's Residence.
123 Zoological Gardens.
FORT WILLIAM
RACE COURSE

W. NEWMAN & CO.'S

HAND-BOOK TO CALCUTTA,

HISTORICAL & DESCRIPTIVE,

WITH A PLAN AND ILLUSTRATIONS.

Calcutta:

W. NEWMAN & CO., 3, DALHOUSIE SQUARE.

1875.

PREFACE.

The want of a Hand-book to Calcutta has long been felt. Residents, as a rule, are but little familiar with its "highways and bye-ways;" and the many associations of the place, connected, as they are, with the rise of the British Power in India, and with the early struggles with an alien race, are lost sight of in the modern pursuit of business and pleasure.

Visitors, for the most part, wander aimlessly through the main streets; seeking in vain for the splendid relics of a past civilisation, and unconscious or forgetful of the mighty changes that a century and a half of English rule have brought about.

The object of this publication is to afford some glimpses of Calcutta in its early state, to trace its progress through reverses, and against odds, that would have crushed the hopes of men less plucky and self-confident than the handful of Englishmen who won India for England; and to describe briefly its present features, incongruous in some respects, but still manifesting in a remarkable degree the power of modern civilisation, and the influence of Western Education.

How imperfectly this object has been accomplished, no one can be more conscious than myself. Material for the purpose abounds, but much time is required for its selection and arrangement, and of this I have had but little at my disposal. As it is, I have made large use of the lectures of the Rev. James Long and Mr. Blochmann on "Calcutta in the olden time"; of the articles of Mr. Long and Mr. Marshman in the *Calcutta Review*, and of such books of early travel and history as are available for the past; and for the present, have relied on such knowledge as I have gained during twenty-four years' residence in Calcutta, aided by the kind contributions of many gentlemen on matters on which they are specially informed, and to whom my best thanks are due.

If I have accomplished nothing more, I may venture to hope that the ground-work has been laid for a fuller and better work on Calcutta, its history, progress, and present state.

A small, but distinct plan of Calcutta, and a few Illustrations of the Principal Buildings, will, it is hoped, add something to the interest of the Book.

JAMES BLACKBURN KNIGHT.

Calcutta, December 1875.

Any emendations or additional information on the subject of Calcutta and its History, will be always gratefully received.

INDEX.

HAND-BOOK TO CALCUTTA.

HISTORICAL INTRODUCTION.

THE first historical notice regarding Calcutta is to be found in the Aín-i-Akbarí, a book written in 1596, by Abul Fazl, the Prime Minister of the Emperor Akbar. We there read that the district of Hooghly, or, as it was then called, the Sirkar of Sátgánw, contained, among others, the three towns of Calcutta, Barbakpur, and Bakúyá, jointly paying into the Imperial Exchequer the annual sum of Rs. 23,405. The name of Calcutta is generally connected with Káli, the Hindu goddess. In books written in the past century, we find the name Calcutta spelt Calicotto, and even Golgota; but the spelling given in the Aín is "Kalkatta," as pronounced by the natives now-a-days.*

* On this subject, the "Indian Antiquary" publishes the following letter:—

"Calcutta is a place known from remote antiquity. The ancient Hindus called it by the name of *Kálikshetra.* It extended from *Bahula* to *Dakhinashar.* *Bahula* is modern *Bahala,* and the site of *Dakhinashar* still exists. According to the *Purânas* a portion of the mangled corpse of *Sati* or *Káli* fell somewhere within that boundary; whence the place was called *Kálikshetra.* Calcutta is a corruption of *Kálikshetra.* In the time of Balâl Sen it was assigned to the descendants of *Sera.*"

PUDMA NAV GHOSAL.

"*Calcutta, July 1873.*"

Calcutta is the sixth Capital in succession which Bengal has had within the last six centuries. 1, *Gaur*, which had flourished for 2,000 years, was deserted and reduced to ruins mainly owing to the shifting of the course of the river; 2, *Rajmahal*, the City of one hundred Kings; 3, *Dhaka* famed from Roman times; 4, *Nuddea*, for five centuries the Oxford of Bengal; 5, *Murshedabad*, the abode of Moslem pride, and the seat of Moslem revelry.

It was during the reign of Aurangzib, on the 20th December, 1686, that the Agent and Council of the English factory at Hooghly, in consequence of a rupture with the Moghul Foujdar stationed there, left Hooghly for Sutanattee (or Chattanattee,) a village on the banks of the river Hooghly, extending from the present Calcutta Mint to Sobha Bazar. The Company's Agent was *Mr. Job Charnock*, who had formerly been chief of the English factory at Casimbazar, near Berhampore. After leaving Hooghly he first tried to establish himself at Oolabaria, 15 miles south of Howrah, but the village of Sutanattee was ultimately preferred.

However, he was not long left in peace, for the Foujdar, having assembled fresh troops, marched down to attack the British encampment, and Job Charnock retired to Hijlee, a low deadly swamp, at the mouth of the river. In three months one-half the troops were dead. New overtures were made by the Viceroy to Charnock, and he returned to Sutanattee; but the Court of Directors sent out reinforcements under Captain Heath, who disallowed the treaty, embarked on board his ships the whole of the Company's Officers at Sutanattee, proceeded down the river, bombarded and burnt Balasore, and finally landed the whole of the Company's establishments at Madras. Subsequently, the Emperor

Aurangzíb, aware that his dominions benefited greatly by the commerce of the English, directed the Viceroy to invite Mr. Charnock to re-establish the Company's factories in Bengal, and offered a compensation of Rs 60,000 for the goods which had been plundered. Charnock embarked for Bengal with the commercial establishments of the Company, and on the 24th August 1690, hoisted the standard of England on the banks of the Hooghly, and laid the foundation of the city of CALCUTTA.

According to Orme's History, Mr. Charnock was a man of courage, without military experience, but impatient to take revenge on the Moghul Government, from whom he had personally received the most ignominious treatment, having been imprisoned and scourged by the mob. This was perhaps the cause of the unwarrantable usage of the natives which has been ascribed to him. According to oral tradition, Charnock built a bungalow at Barrackpore, and a flourishing bazar arose under his patronage before the settlement of Calcutta had been determined upon. Barrackpore is even now-a-days called by the natives *Ohának*, in which word Charnock's name is easily traceable. Charnock died in 1692.

The following account of the settlement of the English at Calcutta is given in Price's Observations :—"When the English first settled at Calcutta, the little body of Merchants, instead of affixing themselves on the west side of the river, as all other Europeans had done before and since, determined on a very *small spot of rising ground* on the east side. If I remember right, their reasons for this choice were, that it was situated near to several populous villages, filled with cloth manufacturers, whom they wished to engage in their service; that they should be free from the invasions of the Mahrattas, who in those days were very troublesome to those settled on the west side of the river; that the anchorage for their ships was very good, and near to the place on which they proposed to erect a little fort; and the ground itself did not cost them much money."

Such reasons may, indeed, have induced Charnock to settle at Sutanattee. History shows that the inhabitants of the western side of the river invariably repaired to Calcutta on the slighest rumour of an approach of the Mahratas. The remark respecting the *rising ground* is also correct; for the ground of old Calcutta *is* high, as any one can see by walking from Clive Street to the river. According to Simm's Survey of Calcutta (in 1851), Clive Street was, in fact, found to be the highest point in the whole modern town of Calcutta, being nearly thirty-one feet above the zero of the tide-gauge at Kidderpore, whilst the lowest part of Calcutta, Machoa Bazar, has a height of eighteen feet only. The high bank of these rivers always has some elevation above the flat inland. The rise of the *old* high bank, now many hundred yards inland, is very perceptible and abrupt as you enter the Burra Bazar from the Strand Road near the Mint.

In 1698 permission was given to put the settlement in a state of defence, and a Fort was ordered to be built, which, in compliment to the reigning Monarch, was named *Fort William*. It occupied the site of Fairlie Place, the Custom House, and Coila Ghat. Its chief defect was the absence of proper ditches round about it. The sides to the east and west extended 210 yards; the southern side 130; the northern side 100; it had four bastions, each mounting ten guns.*

The walls of the old Fort were exposed on digging for the foundations of the Port Commissioners' office, at the corner of Coila Ghat Street and the Strand Road, and, more recently, in laying the foundations for the new East Indian Railway Offices at the corner of Fairlie Place.

In 1700 Prince Azim-ushshán, Aurangzib's grandson, in consideration of a valuable present, permitted the Agents of the East India Company to purchase the three villages with the lands adjacent to their fortified factory, *viz.*, Sutanattee, Calcutta, and Govindpore. These three places extended along the river from Chitpore to Coolie Bazar, the town of Calcutta extending from about 100 yards north of Clive Street to Baboo's Ghat.

The bounderies of Calcutta are thus described by Captain Alexander Hamilton, who visited the City in 1710: "The Company's Colony is limited by a landmark at Governapore (Govindpore) and another near Barnagal (Barnagur) about six miles distant, and the Salt-lake bounds it on the land-side. It may contain in all about 10,000 or 12,000 souls, and the Company's revenues are pretty good and well paid. They rise from Ground-rents and Consulage on all Goods imported and exported by British subjects; but all Natives besides are free from taxes."

In 1707 new privileges were obtained from the Emperor, and Calcutta was declared a separate presidency.

The first permission obtained by the British to trade with

* Its river and land sides are well represented by Daniel, and there are good views of the river front in *Orme's Hindustan* and the *Universal Magazine*, copied by Mr. Long in the *Calcutta Review*, Vol. XVIII.

Bengal was granted about the year 1636, through the influence of a Surgeon named Boughton, who was sent from Surat to Agra to attend on a daughter of the Emperor, Shah Jehan, whom he cured; the second was obtained in 1717, through the solicitation of Mr. Hamilton, Surgeon on the then infant establishment of Fort William. It happened in this wise:

The Nabob Jaffier Khan, having removed the seat of Government from Dhaka to Murshedabad, sought every opportunity of distressing and extorting money from the English, without openly violating the privileges obtained from Aurangzib and Azim-ushshán;—and in 1715 it was decided to despatch an Embassy to Delhi to represent these grievances to the Emperor. The embassy consisted of Messrs. John Surman and Edward Stephenson, two of the ablest factors in the service; an opulent Armenian merchant named Serhand, as interpreter; and Mr. William Hamilton, as surgeon. The embassy, carried presents for the Mogul and his officers valued at £30,000, and arrived at Delhi on the 8th July 1715, after a march of three months; and would in all probability have returned with a civil but empty answer to their petition, but for the following circumstance:

The Emperor Farrukhsiyar had been some time engaged to marry the daughter of Rajah Ajeet Singh, one of the Rajpoot Princes, and the bride had arrived, for that purpose, at the capital, but the Emperor, being afflicted with a complaint which all the skill of his own physicians could not cure, was under the necessity of postponing the marriage. At length, in consequence of the recommendation of Khan Dauran, he permitted Mr. Hamilton, the surgeon of the embassy, to attend him; and that gentleman having, by a judicious operation, restored the Emperor to health, became very deservedly a great favourite with his Majesty, who, in addition to many proofs of the royal munificence, promised to grant him any other favour he should ask. Mr. Hamilton, instead of requesting any further reward for himself, besought his Majesty to concede to the English Ambassadors the object of their mission. The Emperor, surprised at Mr. Hamilton's disinterestedness, promised that, as soon as the marriage ceremonies were over, he would take the petition into his serious consideration, and grant the English every indulgence he could, consistent with the dignity of his own Empire.

Soon after his recovery the marriage of the Emperor took place, but it was not until January 1716 that the Ambassadors could gain permission to present their petition. After a further tedious delay, and with the aid of a little "well-timed bribery," the object of the mission was accomplished, and patents were granted to the British permitting them to purchase thirty-seven villages comprising a district extending ten miles south of Calcutta along the bank on each side of the river Hughly. This concession became a dead letter owing to the opposition of the Nabob Jaffier who deterred the holders, by secret threats of vengeance, from parting with their lands, but certain facilities and immunities were granted which were favorable to the Company's trade, and which possibly were then as highly prized as increase of territory.

"The inhabitants of Calcutta," says Stewart, "enjoyed after the return of the Embassy a degree of freedom and security unknown to the other subjects of the Moghul

Empire; and that city increased yearly in wealth, beauty and riches."

CALCUTTA IN 1717

In 1717, a forest existed to the south of Chandpal Ghat, which was afterwards gradually removed. Between this wood and Kidderpore, on the site of the Esplanade and the present Fort, there were two small villages, the inhabitants of which were invited to settle in Calcutta by the ancient family of the Setts, who were at that time merchants of great note, and very instrumental in bringing Calcutta into the form of a town. In 1717, there was a small village, consisting of straggling huts, surrounded by puddles of water, where now stand the elegant houses of Chowringhee. Between Balliaghat and Calcutta there intervened a jungle, two miles in extent, inhabited by tigers and other ferocious animals.

The office of "*Zamindar*," of Calcutta was created in 1720. He was a judicial functionary who had the entire control of the Municipal, Fiscal, Civil and Criminal affairs of the town, as far as the natives were concerned.

The *Mayor's Court* was established in 1724. It consisted of a Mayor and nine Aldermen, the former elected annually by the latter who were mercantile men, and as a remuneration for their services, enjoyed the magnificent monthly salary of Rs 20. They wore an official garb. The Mayor's Court had jurisdiction in Civil and Criminal matters only over Europeans.

In 1726, Bengal, Madras, and Bombay were created into separate and distinct Presidencies.

Commerce seems, notwithstanding the disadvantages of position, to have grown up early, and with it the usual accompaniment of luxury. In the letters of the Court of Directors, we find frequent complaints and reprobations under this head, and in 1725, Mr. Deane, the President, is severely reproved for having charged "rupees eleven hundred for a chaise and pair" to the public account, which sum he is ordered immediately to refund. "If our servants," say the Directors, "will have such superfluities, let them pay for them."

Despite of reprimands, however, habits of expense continued, and in 1731, we find "the foppery of having a set of music at his table, and a coach and six with guards and running footmen," charged against both the President, and "some of inferior rank;" and as if this were not enough, it is broadly hinted that "wherever such practice prevails in any of our servants, we shall always expect that we are the paymasters in some shape or other."

Captain A. Hamilton, who was in Calcutta in 1710, says, "most gentlemen and ladies in Bengal live both splendidly and pleasantly, the forenoons being dedicated to business, and after dinner to rest, and in the evening to recreate themselves in chaises or *palankins* in the fields, or to gardens, or by water in their *budgeroes*, which are convenient boats that go swiftly by four oars; and on the river sometimes there is the diversion of fishing, or fowling, or both; and before night, they make friendly visits to one another, when pride and contention do not spoil society, which too often they do among the ladies, as discord and faction do amongst the men. And although the conscript fathers of the Colony disagreed in many points among themselves, yet they all agree in oppressing strangers who are consigned to them, not suffering them to buy or sell their goods at the most advantageous markets, but of the Governor and his Council, who fix their own prices, high or low, as seemeth best to their wisdom and discretion.

"The colony has very little manufactory of its own; for the Government being pretty arbitrary, discourages ingenuity and industry in the populace; for by the weight of the Company's authority, if a native chances to disoblige one of the upper-house, he is liable to arbitrary punishment, or corporal sufferings."

Subsequently this wretched state of things seems to have been somewhat improved; for Stewart says, "success produced new adventures, and besides a number of English private merchants licensed by the Company, Calcutta was, in a short time, peopled by Portuguese, Armenian, Mogul, and Hindoo merchants, who carried on their commerce under the protection of the British flag: thus the shipping belonging to the port, in the course of ten years after the Embassy, (that is, the Embassy of 1717) amounted to ten thousand tons, and many individuals amassed fortunes without injury to the Company's trade, or incurring the displeasure of the Mogul Government."

An old Annalist refers to 1737, "as a period when we had opulent merchants, in days when gold was plenty, labour cheap, and not one indigent European in all Calcutta."

The same year brought with it a great calamity. "In the night of the 11th October 1737, there happened a furious hurricane at the mouth of the Ganges, which reached sixty leagues up the river. There was at the same time a violent earthquake, which threw down a great many houses along the river side; in Golgota (*i. e.*, Calcutta) alone, a port belonging to the English, two hundred houses were thrown down, and the high and magnificent steeple of the English Church sunk into the ground without breaking. It is computed that 20,000 ships, barques, sloops, boats, canoes, &c., have been cast away; of nine English ships then in the Ganges, eight were lost, and most of the crews drowned. Barques of sixty tons were blown two leagues up into land over the tops of high trees; of four Dutch ships in the river, three were lost, with their men and cargoes; 300,000 souls are said to have perished. The water rose forty feet higher than usual in the Ganges."—*Gentleman's Magazine*, 1738-9.*

In 1742 the Mahrattas invaded Bengal. They laid waste the country from Balasore to Rajmahal, took Mukwah Tannah Fort, which stood on the site of the house now occupied by the Superintendent of the Botanical Gardens,

---

* To the description of this hurricane there is a very amusing addition, which we quote in the words of the original: "A French ship was driven on shore and bulged; after the wind and the waters abated, they opened their hatches and took out several bales of Merchandise, &c., but the man who was in the hold to sling the bales suddenly ceased working, nor by calling to him could they get any reply; on which they sent down another but heard nothing of him, which very much added to their fear; so that for sometime no one would venture down. At length one more hardy than the rest went down and became silent and inactive as to the two former, to the astonishment of all. They then agreed by lights to look down into the hold, which had a great quantity of water in it, and to their great surprise they saw a huge Alligator staring as if expecting more prey. It had come in through a whole in the ship's side and 'twas with difficulty they killed it, when they found the three men in the creature's belly." ! ! !—*Historical Chronicle*, p. 321.

and finally got possession of Hooghly. The wretched inhabitants took refuge in Calcutta, and the President obtained permission to surround the Company's lands with a ditch, to extend from the northern portion of Sootanuttee to the southern part of Govindpore. In six months three miles were finished, and the work was discontinued—the earth excavated being so disposed on the inner or townward side as to form a road. The ditch was called the *Mahratta Ditch*, and the road the *Circular Road*, upon which, as an old writer states, (in 1802) "the young, the sprightly, and the opulent, during the fragrance of morning, in the Chariot of Health, enjoy the gales of recreation !"

As a means of defence, the ditch was worthless, especially with a small garrison ; and for that reason, probably, it was not used by the English during the attack of Siraj-ud-Dowlah in 1756. It was filled up by order of the Marquis of Wellesley.

In 1748, an account of the alarm excited by the Mahrattas a council was held in Calcutta. In this year Omichand, the Bengali Millionaire, figures for the first time in the annals of Calcutta, as a medium of communication between the English and the Mahrattas. At that time an Anglo-Dutch alliance was formed against the French, and Baranuggar was selected as the port to unload their ships.

In 1750, Mr. Barwell became Governor of Calcutta.

In 1752, The Hon'ble Roger Drake was appointed Governor. The monthly charges of the settlement were about Rs 20,000. The President's salary was Rs 254. A Chaplain received Rs 84 per mensem, and a Doctor Rs 30. But they were allowed liberal Commissions on Merchandise, which paid them handsomely.

In 1753, the Militia mustered 200 strong.

We come now to the great crisis in the History of Calcutta, and, we may say, of India.

In 1756, Alli Virdy, the Viceroy of Bengal, (commonly known as the *Nawab Nazim)* died, and was succeeded by his grandson, Siraj-ud-Dowlah, a youth of twenty, cruel and profligate, and full of implacable hatred to the English. The circumstance of Mr. Drake, the Governor of Calcutta, giving shelter to Kissen Dass, the son of the Governor of Dacca, whose wealth the Viceroy coveted, was made the pretext by Siraj-ud-Dowlah for hostilities. He first demanded the surrender of Kissen Dass, then that the fortifications of Calcutta should be destroyed; and neither of these demands being complied with, he, on the 17th June 1756, marched to Calcutta with an army of 50,000 men. Calcutta was wholly unprepared for such an attack. The fortifications had been utterly neglected, and warehouses were built up to the ramparts which were commanded by the church and adjoining houses. They had not sufficient powder, and what they had was not good. They had hardly any shells fitted, and there was hardly a carriage that would bear a gun. The garrison consisted of "145 men in battalion, and 45 of the train, officers included, and in both only 60 Europeans. There were not five that had ever seen a musket fired in anger. From the Militia about 65, chiefly Europeans, (most of them covenanted servants) entered volunteers in the battalion. In the last struggle, the number engaged on one side did not exceed 170 men, of whom 25 were killed, and about 70 wounded. —*(Holwell's Narrative.)* The senior officers had no military experience or talent, and, consequently, although many of the Civilians and junior Military officers displayed British pluck of the highest order, the troops were almost undisciplined. After much gallant but irregular fighting at temporary outposts, which needlessly divided the small force, the factory was invested. The Fort was not tenable; and a general and orderly retreat might have been effected had those highest in authority possessed the will and judgment to do their duty. Unhappily this was not the case. A Council of War was held, and it was resolved to send the women and children on board the vessels lying off the town. One lady alone, Mrs. Carey, the wife of a ship Captain refused to leave her husband. Two Members of Council, Messrs. Manningham and Frankland, escaped under pretence of escorting the ladies. The embarkation was conducted without order or discipline, and the Captains immediately weighed anchor and dropped down the river to Garden Reach. At 10 in the morning only two boats remained at the wharf, into one of which the Governor, Mr. Drake, quietly slipped. Mr. Mackett, the Commandant Captain Minchin, and Captain Grant followed his example, and rowed down to the ships in all haste. After this base desertion, Mr. Holwell, one of the Company's surgeons, who had long been Zemindar (Collector) of Calcutta, who now commanded the Militia, and whose merits twice raised him to the dignity of Governor of Bengal, was, by common consent, placed in command. He, personally, had every opportunity of escape, but he resolved to defend the Fort until either the shipping might come up the river, or the *St. George* might drop down to enable them to make a general retreat. The *St. George* grounded on a sand bank. Holwell maintained his ground, fighting to the utmost, from the morning of the 19th until late in the afternoon of the 20th, when, he having begun to parley and ceased firing, the enemy swarmed in, aided by the treachery of some of those in the Fort. The Nawab summoned Mr. Holwell before him, reproached him with defending the place against the rightful ruler of Bengal, but assured him that no harm should be done to the prisoners. That evening, however, the whole of them, 146 in number, were crammed into a wretched dungeon, with two small apertures, which had been used as the prison of the garrison, and was called the "Black-hole."* It was one of the hottest nights of the most sultry season of the year, and the wretched prisoners soon became frantic with suffocating heat and insufferable thirst. One by one they sank into the arms of death, and when the door was opened in the morning only 23 came out alive, and they were a fearful spectacle. Mr. Holwell was one of the survivors, and was, by the Nawab's order, kept in confinement.

During the stay of Siraj-ud-Dowlah at Calcutta, he ordered that the town should henceforth be called 'Alinagur.'

Information of this catastrophe was seven weeks in reaching Madras, where Clive was Governor of Fort St. David, and Watson, Admiral of the Fleet; and after some delay, they sailed from Madras on the 10th October, with

* The Black-Hole was a space, 18 feet square, partitioned off from the south end of the barrack. It only became "a wretched dungeon," when it was made to contain a great many people; it was well enough for one or two prisoners. A contemporary writer, cited in Howitt's History of England, said that the cruelty of the English was visited upon themselves. This was not just. The prisoners had precisely the same accommodation as the troops; the prisoners of two companies would never be numerous.

five ships of war and five of the Company's Vessels bearing the army, consisting of 900 Europeans and 1,500 Sepoys, which was destined to effect a mighty revolution in India.

On the 15th December the expedition reached Fulta, where Mr. Drake and the other fugitives were lying in the vessels on which they had taken refuge. A Mogul fortification on the river at Budge-Budge was soon after taken. Clive advanced on Calcutta, and on the 2nd January 1757 re-occupied the town, and the Fort surrendered at discretion. When the news of these transactions reached the Nawab, he marched down from Murshidábád towards Calcutta with an army of 40,000 men. A battle followed, and the Nawab made overtures of peace, and on the 9th February a treaty was concluded, by which all their former privileges were restored to the English, permission was given to fortify Calcutta, and to establish a Mint, and a promise of compensation for losses was held out. But the capture of Chandernagore by the combined forces of Watson and Clive, on the 22nd March, after a siege of nine days, incensed the Nawab, and hostilities were renewed. Clive wrote a peremptory letter to the Nawab, demanding satisfaction for all injuries. The Nawab instantly put his army in motion, and the hostile armies met on the field of PLASSEY. On the 23rd June 1757, the battle was fought. The victory was immediate and decisive, Siraj-ud-Dowlah fled, his army dispersed, and Meer Jaffir, the Commander-in Chief, who had been tampered with by Clive, declared in favour of the English, and with his troops joined their standard. Clive entered Murshidábád on the 29th June, conducted Meer Jaffir to the throne, and saluted him as Soobadar of Bengal, Bihar, and Orissa. The Nawab Siraj-ud-Dowlah, was put to death in prison ; Mahmedy Beg hacking his body into innumerable pieces with a talwar. In accordance with the terms of the treaty, the sum of two crores and twenty lakhs of rupees was gradually paid out of the treasury at Murshidábád, to make good the losses of the Company and of individuals. Clive was then made Governor of the Company's settlements in Bengal. In 1760 he sailed for England.

When Clive and Watson re-took Calcutta in 1757, seven months after the sack, they found some of the best houses of the English demolished or damaged by fire. Old St. John's lay in ruins. The Armenian and Portuguese Churches seem to have escaped. Everything of value belonging to the inhabitants had of course been removed. In the native town, also, many houses lay in ruins. The Burra Bazar had been burnt down. In the middle of the Fort a Mosque had been erected with the material of several buildings which had been pulled down to make room for it. Of the inhabitants of the native town, most of whom had fled at the approach of Siraj-ud-Dowlah ; about 50,000 are said to have afterwards returned. They were, however, mostly of the lower classes, as the rapacity of Manikchand, whom Siraj-ud-Dowlah had left as Governor of Calcutta, deterred such as were known to have property from trusting themselves within his reach. The greater part of the merchandise belonging to the Company, which was stored up in the Fort, was found untouched, for this part of the plunder had been reserved for the Nawab.

According to treaty the English inhabitants of Calcutta recovered fifty, the Hindoo and Mahomedans twenty, and the Armenians seven lakhs of rupees, restitution-money. On the 6th July, about a year after the sack of Calcutta, there arrived from Murshidábád nearly seventy-six lakhs of rupees of coined silver, packed in 700 chests and laden in 100 boats. Never before did the English nation obtain such a prize in solid money. Before another six weeks, forty lakhs more of coined silver arrived in Calcutta, to meet the losses sustained by the Company. The treaty permitted the Company to establish a mint, from which the first coin was issued on the 19th August, 1757. The coins were, however, struck in the name of the Emperor of Delhi. It was not till the reign of William IV. that the Company commenced to strike rupees with the King's head and an English inscription.

This treaty increased the territory of Calcutta by 600 yards beyond the ditch, and contained also the grant of the 24-Pergunnahs.* Immediately after the receipt of the restitution-money, a committee of the most respectable inhabitants was appointed to distribute the money. They executed the office with much discretion and equity. Commerce revived; the destroyed houses were re-built; in fact, we may date modern Calcutta from 1757. The present Fort William was commenced; the inhabitants of the native village situated between Chowringhee and the river got notice to quit, and thus arose our *Maidan*, "the lungs of Cal-

* The quit-rent or Government share of these Pergunnahs, amounting to Rupees 2,22,000 annually, was conferred by the Mogul on Lord Clive, and was paid to him until his death, which took place in November, 1774, when it reverted to the Company. In 1759, the Pergunnahs were farmed out for three years certain, resulting in a nett annual revenue to the Company of 6,93,700 Sicca Rupees, after deducting Lord Clive's Jaghire. The superficial area of the district is 2,277 square miles.

cutta," as it has been styled. The formation of the airy maidan caused the European inhabitants gradually to shift their dwellings eastward; and whilst, before 1756, the neighbourhood of Tank Square was the fashionable quarter; it afterwards became the place for Mercantile and Government Offices. The demolition of the Old Fort left the Company in possession of a large piece of ground which was used for public buildings. Its demolition was gradually and slow. Daniell's views, *Cir.* 1770, show a complete exterior. It was employed for civil purposes, when the new fort was completed. Nearly the whole of the southern piazza of the old building remains, and has been accurately represented in the *Illustrated London News.*

The year 1757, distinguished by the glorious success of the British arms in India, was also marked by one of the fearful epidemics which formerly characterised Bengal, when patients were carried off after a cold stage of twelve hours. The former insalubrity of Calcutta was so great, that, up to the end of the last century, the European inhabitants of Calcutta used to meet on the 15th of November, each year, to congratulate each other on their escape from the rainy season and the effluvia of the Salt Lakes.

In 1765, Lord Clive returned to Calcutta, and assumed the reins of Government on the 7th May. On the 12th of August he obtained for the East India Company, from the Emperor of Delhi, the Dewaní of Bengal, Behar and Orissa, agreeing to pay a tribute of two lakhs of Rupees per annum.

Another grievous famine and pestilence occurred in 1770,* which affected Bengal generally, and carried off,

* Martin's Medical Topography of Calcutta.

according to Mr. Hickey, 76,000 souls in the streets of Calcutta, between the 15th July and the 10th September. In addition to this calamity, several great granaries were destroyed by terrible fires, which took place in May and June of that year.

Stavorinus, the Dutch Admiral, who was in Bengal about this time, thus writes :—"These poor people (the Bengalees) who contribute so much to the prosperity of the country instead of being favoured and encouraged by the English, are, on the contrary, continually exposed to the rapacious extortions of their taskmasters, and are oppressed in every way, partly by open violence, and partly by monopolies, which the English have made of all articles necessary to life,—the dried cow-dung not excepted, which these poor people use for fuel. But this is not so much to be ascribed to the English Company, as to their servants, who leave no means untried to accumulate wealth. They do not trouble themselves about the manner of obtaining it, so they do but speedily amass the riches they are in search of. Instead of preventing these monopolies, which were, in a great measure, the cause of the scarcity of provisions which was felt in the spring of 1770, the English Government at Calcutta suffer them to exist unnoticed and unremedied ; and it has in consequence, not been improbably suspected, that they are themselves concerned in these iniquitous transactions."*

---

* Stavorinus was a jealous Dutchman. No colonists were ever more oppressive than the Dutch. The English Company must have given a strong impulse to trade (not to *Dutch* monopolies) in Bengal. Their mode of carrying on the rice trade was not immaculate, but to attribute the famine to the English is absurd.

In fact, the Proprietors and Directors of the East India Company were essentially partners and managers of a trading establishment, and nothing could console them for insufficient dividends. The servants of the Company neglected their duties, and only made haste to be rich.

To give an example. In 1765, a private Company was formed in Calcutta, among the servants of the Honorable East India Company (Lord Clive included,) for the purpose of establishing a monopoly of salt, betel-nut, tobacco, &c. There were 60 shares, and the shareholders were the rulers of the country! The Directors at home put a stop to it; but as the communication with England was very slow, the Company existed for two years, during which the shareholders had a clear profit of nearly eleven lakhs of rupees. Nor was it Europeans alone who made their fortunes. A Muhammedan writer mentions the examples of Ram Chand, the Dewan, and of Nobo Krishna, Clive's Munshi. The former left twelve and a half millions of rupees at his death, in 1767; and Nobo Krishna could afford to pay nine lakhs of rupees on the occasion of the death of his mother, although both men were, in 1757, in receipt of only sixty rupees per month.

The magnitude of the fortunes realised may be contrasted with the magnitude of the dreadful famine of 1770. Already, in 1768 and 1769, the crops had proved scanty; in October 1769, scarcely a drop of rain fell; and in 1770 the famine at last set in. The high-ways and fields were strewed with the dying and the dead. The water and the fishes of the Hooghly became unfit for use. Rice sold at four seers for the rupee, and was at last no longer to be had. Mutton is said to have been the only article that could be eaten in safety : all other meats had become poisonous. More than three millions of inhabitants appear to have been cut off in Bengal. Like the late famine in Orissa, Bengal and Madras it produced a great stir at home, especially because the French in Chandernagore had spread the calumny that the servants of the Company had bought up the whole rice crop of the country, and had resorted to the inhuman expedient of an artificial famine, in order to establish a monopoly of grain.

In 1773, Parliament determined to interfere, for the better regulation of the British territories in the East Indies. The Charter of the Company was renewed, with some important changes in its constitution, and the following provisions added :—

(1.) That £400,000 a year should be paid by the Company to the nation.

(2.) That the Governor of Calcutta should become Governor-General, with a salary of £25,000 a year ; and, assisted by a Council, should be supreme over all the British possessions in India.

(3.) That a Supreme Court of Judicature, consisting of a Chief Justice and three other Judges, should be established in Calcutta.

The great mistake in the Regulating Act was, that *the four Members of the Governor-General's Council were to have equal authority in Council with himself.*

Warren Hastings was appointed first Governor-General in October, 1774, on a salary of two and a half lakhs of rupees per annum, and held this high office for eleven years, "thwarted and misrepresented by the selfishness of the East India Company in England and by the miserable perverseness of his colleagues in India." His colleagues were Colonel Monson, General Clavering, Mr. Francis, (afterwards Sir Phillip Francis) and Mr. Barwell, senior Member. The last, who had been long in India, invariably supported Mr. Hastings; the other three as pertinaciously opposed him: and as the votes of the majority decided every matter, the new Governor-General found himself shorn of all power by his accession of dignity. Hastings struggled against them with wonderful firmness and with occasional errors of judgment, till the end of 1780, when Francis left the country. Monson died in 1776, and Clavering in 1777. Sir Eyre Coote succeeded the latter.

Perhaps the event which created the most profound sensation at this period, and which formed the principal ground of accusation against Hastings on his trial, was the execution of Nund Kumar. The Maharaja Nund Kumar belonged to the highest order in the Brahman caste. His distinguished abilities, address, and knowledge procured him the unbounded confidence of the Murshidábád Darbar, from which position he intrigued against the British Government. Suspicion falling upon him, he was arrested and sent down to Calcutta in October, 1774. Here he became the tool and spy of the Council, and in this capacity he preferred certain accusations against Hastings, which were transparently false and supported by palpable forgeries.

While this was going on, Nund Kumar was arrested on a charge of forgery, tried in the Supreme Court, and sentenced to be hanged. The execution took place publicly at Kuli Bazar, on the 5th August, 1775 "within a few paces off Fort William." More than a hundred thousand natives surrounded the scaffold, believing that there was no intention of hanging him; but when they saw him actually executed, they ran down with one accord to the river, to wash out the pollution. It is said that many Brahminical families immediately settled upon the opposite side of the river, founding Balakhal and Uterparah.

Mackintosh writes: "This answered all the purpose of the conspirators; the charge against the Governor-General dropt, and no native of India has dared to hint a censure against an European Member of Government in Hindustan ever since."

The Supreme Court, which was instituted in 1774, "to protect natives from oppression, and to give India the benefits of English law," is described by Mackintosh (writing in 1772) in the following trenchant style:—"The present mode of administering justice, under the sanction of a British Act of Parliament, in Bengal, is a subject which calls loudly for public attention and speedy relief. This dreadful evil threatens the extinction of the British power and property in India. Corruption hath usurped the sacred seat of justice, and, shielded by the power of a venal government, hath held quiet possession of this station for six lingering years, without even the veil of hypocrisy to shade the horrors of oppression and savage violence." * * "The mention of one circumstance, (he continues) may alone suffice to give an idea of the rapacity of the Supreme Court of Judicature in Bengal, and of the deplorable state of that country, over which it extends its iniquitous jurisdiction. On a medium computation, it has been found, that the fees of processes and writs issuing from the Supreme Court have amounted annually to the enormous sum of four hundred and twenty-six thousand pounds sterling. What must be the entire sum which, according to this specimen, is exacted by the several members of this arbitrary and oppressive Court ?"*

"The Court," says another writer, "interfered between the zemindars and their ryots. The attorneys stirred up strife everywhere. Every thing was to be brought under the jurisdiction of the Supreme Court. They applied English ideas to Indian affairs in an undiscriminating spirit."

Hastings proposed a remedy: there was a Court of Appeal in Calcutta, called the Sudder Dewanny Adalut, presided over by the Governor-General and his Council. Hastings offered the appointment of Chief Judge of this Court to Sir Elijah Impey, the Chief Justice of the Supreme Court. This reconciled all parties, and enabled Impey to turn his attention to the subject of the administration of justice according to such forms as might suit the greater simplicity of native habits. Though subsequently disallowed by the Directors, this is the system which came in force in 1860 by the amalgamation of the Supreme Courts in each Presidency with the Company's Courts of Appeal. The Chief Justice now directs the whole judicial system in each Presidency, as Hastings desired.

Hastings held office for eleven years. For the following twenty months Sir John Macpherson, Senior Member of Council, acted as Governor-General, and in 1786 the Marquis of Cornwallis was appointed. His mission was to be that of a peace-maker and reformer. His firmness repressed

* No *proof* of extortion here. Still no profession in India pays so well as the Law. The only thing in which the natives spend freely is in Law process. An English Barrister would be surprised to learn that the position of a leading Counsel here is worth from Rs 10,000 to Rs 15,000 a month.

the factions, and he bent all his energies to the removal of corruption from all branches of the service. Such a reform was never more needed. At this time small salaries were given to the Company's servants, consequently the service did not attract the best men, and contained many from whom nothing better could have been expected; and as their opportunities were great, they easily yielded to the temptation of enriching themselves by every species of official depredation.

His first effectual measure of reform was that of assigning to every officer of Government such a salary as should leave him no manner of excuse for trading, or attempting to acquire money by corrupt practices. This measure, added to an incomparable firmness and consistency in resisting all jobbery and favouritism, and in punishing all frauds, soon cleansed the Augean stable. The purity of the Indian services soon became (and has continued to be) as conspicuous as their corruption had been notorious. To Lord Cornwallis is also due the measure known as the Permanent Settlement. Lord Cornwallis resigned in 1793, and was succeeded by Sir John Shore (afterwards Lord Teignmouth.)

The Marquis of Wellesley, "*the Akbar of the Company's Dynasty*," arrived in India in May 1798, and quitted it in August, 1805. He was a man of genius refined by education, and of large and comprehensive mind, and under his rule, supported, as he was, by a circle of men of remarkable ability, both in the civil and military services, both Calcutta and the country at large prospered.

The commencement of the present century found Calcutta steadily progressing in the path of material improvement, of which we shall treat more fully when we come to describe Calcutta, as it is, and to trace its progress. A few notes are subjoined descriptive of Calcutta, as it appeared to visitors in the last century.

* Speaking of the early English settlers, Price says :—"Round their little fort and close to it, by degrees they built themselves very neat, useful, if not elegant houses, a church, a court-house, &c., laid out walks, planted trees, and made their own little district neat, clean, and convenient." The houses, however, were without flues, venetians, glass windows or punkahs ; they had panelled doors only, and frames with a net-work of cane for windows. "Carriages they had none, for there were no carriage roads then in the country, nor for many years after." "The then town," says Hamilton, "was built without order, as the builders thought most convenient for their own affairs, everyone taking in what ground best pleased them for gardening, so that in most houses you must pass through a garden into a house ; the English building near the river-side and the natives within land."

† Grandpére, who visited Bengal in 1789, writers :—"As we enter the town, a very extensive square opens before us, with a large piece of water in the middle for the public use. The pond has a grass plot round it, and the whole is enclosed by a wall breast-high, with a railing on the top. The sides of this enclosure are each nearly five hundred yards in length. The square itself is composed of magnificent houses, which render Calcutta not only the handsomest town in Asia, but one of the finest in the world. One side of the square consists of a range of buildings occupied by

* Census Report of Calcutta, by H. Beverley, C. S., 1876.

† Ibid.

persons in civil employments under the Company, such as writers in the public offices. Part of the side towards the river is taken up by the old fort, which was the first citadel built by the English after their establishment in Bengal."

CALCUTTA IN 1780, ACCORDING TO MACKINTOSH.

"There are few circumstances of a public character that are more disreputable to the conduct of the English in India than the plan and general government of the town of Calcutta in Bengal. * * *

"It is a truth that from the Western extremity of California to the Eastern Coast of Japan, there is not a spot where judgment, taste, decency, and conveniency are so grossly insulted, as in that scattered and confused chaos of houses, huts, sheds, streets, lanes, alleys, windings, gutters, sinks, and tanks, which, jumbled into an undistinguished mass of filth and corruption, equally offensive to human sense and health, compose the capital of the English Company's Government in India. The very small portion of cleanliness which it enjoys is owing to the familiar intercourse of hungry jackals by night, and ravenous vultures, kites, and crows by day. In like manner it is indebted to the smoke raised in public streets, in temporary huts and sheds, for any respite it enjoys from mosquitoes,—the natural production of stagnated and putrid waters."*

MACKINTOSH'S SCHEME FOR ITS IMPROVEMENT.

"Whatever plan shall be adopted for establishing a proper police in Calcutta, may be carried into execution by a con-

* Mackintosh might have saved himself all this description, and have said that it was a native town. Nothing that *we* laid out or built was filthier than London at that period.

stitutional body, consisting of the Governor-General, the Supreme Council of the Indies, and a certain limited number of persons, properly qualified, and elected by the free and copy-holders of Calcutta, to represent them for these special purposes in general assembly. These three estates should be invested with legislative powers, sufficient for enacting laws for resuming, selling, throwing down, re-building, repairing, lengthening, widening, cleansing, draining, and doing everything consistent with justice to individuals, that may be necessary for building houses, making streets, squares, tanks, drains, and establishing a regular police within the city and precincts of Calcutta; and also assessing and levying taxes, duties, and imposts on the inhabitants thereof, for these purposes."

The future Seat of Government.

"In the choice of the object in question, strict regard should be had to situation, water-communication, elevation, and air. Upon the banks of the Hooghly, from Kedgeree to Cossim-Bazar, there is not so eligible a spot as that pitched upon by the representatives of the late French East India Company at Chandernagore. The elevation of that town is such, that all the rain which falls in and around it will nearly convey itself, at all seasons of the year and tides, without obstruction into the river. Its situation is even, its air clear, dry, and salubrious. Its soil contains such a large proportion of sand, as to render it fertile by instantly absorbing the rain. The river Hooghly is navigable to Chandernagore by a third-rate man-of-war * * but it is not navigable for a vessel of any considerable size half a league higher up; a circumstance, by the way, which may give rise to an idea of facilitating the communication between Calcutta and Chandernagore, by a *stone or wooden bridge (!)* over the river below Chinsurah. Various advantages in point of security, revenue, and expediency, might arise from this communication, in which a draw-bridge should be made over one of the arches at each side, for the passage of large or masted vessels, as well as for occasional defence."

Grandpére, who was here in 1790, gives a frightful account of the drainage and conservancy of the town. The only drains were "open canals," into which dead carcases and every kind of abomination were thrown and left to putrify, and the only scavengers were the jackals and birds of prey. The plague of flies was insupportable ; and, as for the musquitoes, he says, "they beset one so obstinately, are so easily provoked, and so extremely insatiable, that too many precautions cannot be taken against them. To be secure from their attacks, it is the custom to wear within doors, if one stays any time, whether for meals or any other purpose, pasteboard about the legs."

Probably these descriptions refer mainly to the "Black Town," (as it is sometimes called) or the Northern Division, which is chiefly inhabited by natives,—and the writers may not have seen so much of the Southern Division as did Viscount Valentia, who during his visit here in 1803, was *fêted* by the Magnates of the land as a nobleman should be. We may presume also that considerable improvements had taken place in ten years. He says :

"The town of Calcutta is at present well worthy of being the seat of our Indian Government, both from its size, and from the magnificent buildings which decorate the part of it inhabited by Europeans. The citadel of Fort William is a very fine work, but greatly too large for defence. The Esplanade leaves a grand opening, on the edge of which is placed the new Government House, erected by Lord Wellesley, a noble structure, although not without faults in the architecture, and, upon the whole, not unworthy of its destination. * * On a line with this edifice is a range of excellent houses, chunamed and ornamented with verandahs.

"Chowringhee, an entire village of palaces, runs for a considerable length at right-angles with it, and altogether forms the finest view I ever beheld in any city."

This is saying a good deal for a perfectly flat plain, but it may be said with truth, that no one can look south from the upper verandah of the High Court or from Government House without being charmed with the prospect.

"The Black Town," continues our Author, "is as complete a contrast to this as can well be conceived. Its streets are narrow and dirty; the houses, of two stories, occasionally brick, but generally mud, and thatched, perfectly resembling the cabins of the poorest class in Ireland."*

---

* His Lordship took a very superficial view of the Black Town, and knew very little of the rich Bengali's mode of lodging himself. This worthy did not care for what we consider the advantages of open frontage. He was not anxious to erect his mansion in a wide street or open compound, where his women would not be secluded, where the dacoits would find him out, and where his employer would remark, "You must be growing rich. Your mansion is twice as fine as mine!" He, therefore, always faced his property with mean huts occupied by artizans who paid remarkably well; and you can still only approach his double quadrangle by a lane almost as narrow and tortuous as a rabbit burrow, but which is cool, damp, shaded in the hottest weather, and which could be strongly barricaded at the shortest notice.

This portion of the town has been greatly improved of late years; but there are still many abominations to be removed, and much to be done before we can be said to have introduced all the benefits of western civilization into our fair city.

CALCUTTA IN THE OLDEN TIME.

Its Localities.

The period in the history of Calcutta of which we write is one but little beyond the memory of living men. We have described its appearance a hundred and fifty years ago, just struggling, as it were, into being. We have passed the great crisis in its history, from which date, it may be said, our Indian Empire commenced, and our object now is mainly to describe such localities as serve to connect the past with the present. For the details of this we are greatly indebted to the Rev. James Long's interesting contributions to the *Calcutta Review*.

Garden Reach commences at the southerly boundary of the port and extends north to Kidderpore. It appears to have been in its glory in 1780. Mrs. Fay, writing in that year says: "The banks of the river are studded with elegant mansions called garden houses. These houses are surrounded with groves and lawns, which descend to the waters' edge, and present a constant succession of whatever can delight the eye, or bespeak wealth and elegance in the owners." In 1857, the residence of the Ex-King of Oudh was fixed at Garden Reach, in the beautiful house and grounds formerly occupied hy Sir Lawrence Peel. Much of the adjoining property has been bought up by the King,

E

as a consequence, this beautiful suburb has become less popular as a residence for Europeans.

*Kidderpore.**—Here, in 1780, Colonel Henry Watson established wet and dry docks, and a marine yard for repairing and equipping vessels of war and merchantmen. The next year he launched the *Nonsuch* frigate of 36 guns, and in 1788 the *Surprise* frigate of 36 guns. For eight years he devoted his time and fortune to this national undertaking, by which time he had sunk ten lakhs of Rupees in his enterprise, and was obliged to abandon it, his resources being exhausted. The docks afterwards fell into the hands of the two East Indian sons of Colonel Kyd, an enterprising European, the Chief Engineer on the E. I. Company's Military establishment. In 1818, they launched from the dock the *Hastings*, a 74 gun-ship. Between 1781 and 1800, thirty-five vessels were launched; from 1781 to 1821, the total was 237, at a cost of more than two millions sterling. At Fort Gloucester, about 5 miles below, on the opposite side of the river, between 1811 and 1828, 27 vessels were built; and there was also a dock-yard at Titaghur, near Barrackpore, at which in 1801, a vessel of 1,445 tons, the *Countess of Sutherland*, was built. Kyd's dock-yard is now the Government dock-yard, but for many years no vessels of any size have been built there.

In the east part of Kidderpore is the *Military Orphan School*, established in 1783, by Major Kirkpatrick. The fine Ball-room in this building calls to mind the state of society in former days, when European ladies were afraid to face the climate of India. In consequence, Kidderpore was a harbour of refuge, where men in want of wives made their se-

* The correct orthography is said to be Khetter-pore.

lection, at balls given expressly for that purpose, travelling often a distance of 500 miles down the country to attain that object. But *tempora mutantur.*

North of Kidderpore, and separating it from the Maidan, flows *Tolly's Nullah* or canal excavated by Colonel Tolly in 1775, at his own expense. It was formerly known as the Govindpore creek, and was, in fact, part of the old bed of the Ganges, which, washing the steps of the temple to Siva, several centuries old, which formerly stood to the south of the Presidency Jail, proceeded past Tollygunge and Kalighat. It now runs into the Circular Canal, which again communicates with the Hooghly, north of Chitpore, forming the great inlet for country boats bringing produce from the Sunderbunds and the Eastern districts of Bengal.

The temple of *Kalighat* probably stood for centuries, when the Ganges itself, some miles wide, laved its walls, when human blood streamed on its altars, and when Thugs, before proceeding on their expeditions, made their devoirs to Kali.

Crossing Tolly's Nullah by the Hastings Bridge,* a fine, suspension bridge erected by the subscriptions of the community to commemorate the administration of the Marquis of Hastings, we come to *Coolie Bazar.*† It is now the place where the Non-commissioned Officers connected with the Ordnance and Commissariat Departments chiefly reside, and where the Government Commissariat Godowns are situated. It was here that Nunda Kumar, Dewan to the Nawab of

* The bridge suddenly collapsed in 1874, but a new and substantial one has been erected.

† The numerous workmen and coolies employed in building the fort are said to have formed a regular colony to the south, and given rise to the name—Coolie Bazar.

Moorshedabad, was executed, August 5th, 1755, the first Bráhman hanged by the English in India. The name of the place is now changed to *Hastings.*

Proceeding east, the Nullah is crossed by another bridge, called the Kidderpore Bridge. Still further east, is the Zeerut Bridge, leading to *Belvedere,* once the favourite residence of Warren Hastings. The house was the property of Sir Charles Imhoff, son of the Baroness Imhoff, (subsequently Mrs. Hastings) who occupied a house outside the grounds, still known as Hastings House. Mrs. Fay thus describes Belvedere in 1780:—

"The house is a perfect *bijou;* most superbly fitted up with all that unbounded affluence can display; but still deficient in that simple elegance which the wealthy so seldom attain. The grounds are said to be very tastefully laid out."

Belvedere was sold to Mr. Charles Prinsep, Advocate General, who resided there many years, from whom it was purchased by Govenment; it has since been greatly enlarged and improved, and is now the official residence of the Lieutenant-Governor of Bengal.*

Returning to the Circular Road leading from the Zeerut Bridge, we pass the old *Sudder Dewanny Adalut,* or Appeal Court, now used as the Military Hospital. It was originally

---

* A friend supplies the following note, "on good authority," which gives a somewhat different account to the above:—

"Hastings lodged the Baron and Baroness Imhoff in a small dwelling, part of the walls of which still exist in Belvedere House. He lived near, and cultivated the intimacy. Hastings used to cross the plain in a palkee, and the nullah in a dinghee. Hastings never lived on the site of the present Belvedere. Where he did live in that neighbourhood is, I think, a question which needs sifting."

built as a Hospital for the sick of the Regiment in the Fort, and most admirably planned for the purpose; but as soon as it was completed, Lord W. Bentinck "utilised" it as a Court. It has been restored to its proper use within the last few years.

The *General Hospital* adjoining, was established in the year 1768. It was originally a garden-house and was purchased by Government and converted into a hospital.

We enter Chowringhee road from the south. This is the main road from Chitpore to Kalighat. The splendid maidan to the west was formerly a dense jungle. It was commenced to be cleared in 1757. The whole district to the east is of modern erection. Upjohn, in his Map, issued in 1794, places only 24 houses in Chowringhee; and a lady still* living recollects when there were only two houses in Chowringhee—one Sir Elijah Impey's, the very building now occupied as Loretto House Convent. On the site of the adjoining church was a tank, called the *Gol Talao;* the surrounding quater was Sir E. Impey's park, which was surrounded by a fine wall, and stretched from Chowringhee Road on the west to Park Street on the north, an avenue of trees leading from his house, through what is now Middleton Row into Park Street. The other house is the one adjoining the Imperial Museum, formerly occupied as St. Paul's School, now the Bengal office.

Park Street, (native name Badámtolla or Almond grove) so called, because it led to Sir E. Impey's park, is mentioned in Upjohn's Map (1794) by the name of "Burial-

* This was written in 1852. The lady alluded to is doubtless Mrs. Ellerton who died about 1857 at the age of upwards of 80, and whose recollections as to early times in Calcutta were remarkably clear.

ground road," as it was the route for burials from town to the Circular road burial ground : hence it was dreaded as a residence.

In a house at the corner of Wood Street and Theatre Road, formerly occupied by the Eye Infirmary, lived *Colonel Stewart*, commonly known as Hindu Stewart, from his conformity to idolatrous customs. He was one of a class, now passed away, who looked with almost equal regard on the worship of Christ and Krishna.

At the corner of Park Street is the *Asiatic Society's House*, built on a piece of ground granted by Government. The Society was founded in 1784. The house is the property of the Society.

The oldest road on the Maidan is the *Course*, so called as being a coss or two miles in length. It is described in 1768 as being "out of town in a sort of angle, made to take the air in," though an old song states that those who frequented it, "swallowed ten mouthfuls of dust for one of fresh air." It is still one of the airest and pleasantest drives in Calcutta, extending from the "Cocked Hat" on the north to the Kidderpore Bridge. The broad gravelled walk on the west side, called Secretary's Walk, was constructed in 1820. On the right is the *Ellenborough Course*, a fine raised and turfed ride for horse exercise ; and towards the South the *Race Course*, commenced in 1819.

The direct road from Park Street to Government House, known as the "Bentinck Road," is said to have been made to enable Dr. Simon Nicholson, who lived and died in the house now occupied by the United Service Club, to have ready access to Government House.

Dhurrumtollah (properly *Dharmtala)* commences at the

north-end of Chowringhee. It was formerly called *The Avenue*, as it led from the town to the Salt Water Lakes and the adjacent country. Last century it was a "well-raised causeway, raised by deepening the ditch on either side," with wretched huts on the south side. It was shaded with trees on both sides. It derives its name from a great mosque, which formerly stood on the site of Cook's stables. Hence *Dharmtala*, or *Holy Street*. Dhurrumtollah Bazar was established in 1794. It was formerly called Shakespeare's bazar, and it was one of the sites thought of for the new Town Hall.

Just north of Dhurrumtollah, a creek formerly ran from Chandpal Ghat to Ballia Ghat near the Salt Lakes. The creek passed through Wellington Square and Creek Row, and was navigable for large boats. The native name of Creek Row, *Dinga Bhanga*, is said to have its origin in the wrecking at that place of a ship which, during the terrible Cyclone of 1737, had been driven up by a storm wave from the river.

The Creek is represented in an early view copied in Howitt's History of England. It commenced at Coilah Ghat, bounded the Burial Ground, on the south, was crossed by a bridge at the south-east gate of St. John's Church, where there was a redoubt when Calcutta was attacked. Its mouth may have extended from Chandpal to Coilah Ghat.

Cossitollah, or more correctly *Kasaitoli*, now Bentinck Street, leading from Chowringhee Road into old Calcutta, was named after the *Kasâie* or Butchers, who formerly occupied it as their quarter. It must, therefore, have been a hateful street for Hindus to pass through on their way from Chitpore to Kalighat. In 1757 Cossitollah was a mass of jungle, and even as late as 1780 it was almost impassable from mud in the rains. *Grant's Lane* is named after Mr. Charles Grant, father of Lord Glenelg, whose residence was on that spot. At that time there were only two or three houses in the street.

Lal Bazar, in 1768, was said to be the best street in Calcutta. It then stretched from the north-east corner of the Lall Diggee square to Baitakkhana. The *Police Office* was the residence of John Palmer, one of the "Merchant princes" of Calcutta. His father was the Secretary to Warren Hastings. He was noted for his princely hospitality, and on one occasion entertained two Governor-Generals. On the opposite side of the street, stood the old Jail of Calcutta, and the house next to the Police Office, formerly the Sailors' Home, but now occupied as the Magistrate's Court, was the famous *Harmonicon Tavern*, the handsomest house then in Calcutta. Mrs. Fay writes of it in 1780:

"I felt far more gratified some time ago when Mrs. Jackson procured me a ticket for the Harmonic, which was supported by a select number of gentlemen, who, each in alphabetical rotation, give a concert, ball and supper, during the cold season, I believe once a fortnight."

There were many other hotels and houses of entertainment in the street, at one of which, "the London," entertainments were furnished at the *moderate price* of a gold mohur a head, exclusive of dessert and wines. At the coffee houses, a single dish of coffee cost one rupee."

A little to the north is the *Tiretta Bazar*, established about 1788 by a Frenchman of that name who was superintendent of streets and buildings. It yielded a monthly rental of Rs3,000. It is now the property of the Maharajah of Burdwan.

Opposite the site of the *Tiretta Bazar* stood the house of Charles Weston, who was born there in 1731. The house was surrounded by a large garden. This gentleman was the friend and associate of Mr. Holwell, and generously provided for the comfort of his latter days. He had acquired a large fortune, and gave away regularly Rs1600 monthly in charity, and at his death left a sum of one lakh of rupees, the interest of which is still distributed monthly by St. John's Vestry to the poor of Calcutta.

In 1770 we find advertised in "Hickey's Gazette" a house near the Baitakkhana situated to the southward of Mr. Charles Weston's Garden. This was perhaps another garden.

The road from Lall Bazar to the Old Church, called *Mission Row*, was formerly named *the Rope Walk*, and was the scene of hard fighting at the time of the siege of Calcutta in 1757.

Tank Square (now called *Dalhousie Square*) was, last century, "in the middle of the city." It covers upwards of 25 acres of ground. "It was dug by order of Government, to provide the inhabitants of Calcutta with water, which is very sweet and pleasant. The number of springs which it contains makes the water in it almost on the same level. It is railed round, no one may wash in it." *(Stavorinus).* Its first name was "The Green before the Fort. No doubt it was the place of recreation for the Company's factors, and in the middle of last century it was the scene of many a moonlight gambol of young people, and elderly ones too, who, rigged out in stockings of different colours, yellow coat, green waistcoat, &c., &c., amused themselves on the banks of the "fish pond in the park," (as it was then called) inhaling the evening breezes, and talking of the friends of whom they had heard nine months before. The tank was formerly more extensive, but was cleansed and embanked completely in Warren Hastings' time. It has always been esteemed the sweetest water in Calcutta, and until the introduction of the municipal water supply, was the chief source of supply of drinking water to the European community.

Old Court House Street is so called from the Old Court House, or Town Hall, which stood at the northern extremity of the street, at or near the site of St. Andrew's Church. It was erected about 1727, by Mr. Bouchier, a merchant, who was afterwards appointed Governor of Bombay. In 1734 he gave it to Government, on condition of their paying Rs4000 annually to support a charity school. This money is still paid by Government to the Free School. In 1765 it was considerably enlarged by private subscriptions, in consideration of which Government agreed to give Rs. 800 monthly to the school. Over the Court House were two handsome assembly rooms, which were used for balls, meetings, &c. Daniels gives a drawing of the Court House, with elephants walking in Tank Square, for in the last century elephants were permitted to perambulate the town.

Near the Old Court House, in the north-west corner of Lyon's Range, stood the *Theatre*, which, in the siege of 1757, was turned into a battery by the Moors, and annoyed the Fort very much. The Theatre was generally served by amateur performers, and was frequented by the authorities. A ballroom was attached.

Writer's Buildings, occupying the north side of Dalhousie Square, was appropriated for the residence of writers, or young civilians. The buildings were rented by Government from the Barwell family. Mr. Barwell was Governor of Calcutta in 1750, and retired in 1780, on a fortune of eighty lakhs.*

The *College of Fort William*, on its establishment, in 1800, was located in the premises now the Exchange, and in the range of buildings on the other side of Council House Street, formerly the *Hurkaru* office. The two buildings were connected by a gallery across the street.

To the west of Writer's Buildings, stood the first *Church* of Calcutta, called *St. John's* at the suggestion of the Freemasons,† who were liberal contributors to it. It was built in 1716, when "gold was plenty and labour cheap," chiefly by the pious contributions of sea-faring men. This church is said to have been perfect in composition; its steeple was very lofty and uncommonly magnificent. The Governor, every Sunday, *walked* to it in solemn procession, attended by all the servants of the Company and the Military off duty. The steeple fell in the earthquake of 1737, and the church itself was demolished in the siege of 1756.

* A handsome new frontage has been added to this range of buildings which, with the extensive new blocks erected in Lyons Range accommodate all the officers of the Bengal Government.

† We have accounts of a Freemasons' Lodge in Calcutta in 1874. In 1789, they gave at the Old Court House a ball and supper to the Members of the Company's service in Calcutta; and they seem to have had a local habitation and a name there from the days of Charnock. Their institution tended to mitigate the exclusiveness of European caste in former times.

In the north-west corner of Tank Square once stood the *Black-Hole.* Near its site stood an obelisk, 50 feet high, inscribed with the names of the victims who perished in the Black-Hole on the 20th June 1757. It was erected at the expense of Mr. Holwell, but was pulled down by order of the Marquis of Hastings in 1840.

The tablet on the obelisk bore the following inscription:—

To the Memorys of
Edward Eyre and William Baillie, Esqs. ; the Revd. Jervus Bellamy ; Messrs. Jenks, Reevely, Law, Coates, Nahcourt, Jebb, Torriano, E. Page, S. Page, Grub, Street, Harod, P. Johnstone, Ballard, N. Drake, Carse, Knapton, Gosling, Dod, and Dalrymple ; Captains Clayton, Buchanan, and Witherington ; Lieutenants Bishop, Hays, Blagge, Simpson, and J. Bellamy ; Ensigns Paccard, Scott, Hastings, C. Wedderburn, and Dymbleton ; Sea-captains Hunt, Osburn, and Purnell ; Messrs. Carey, Leech, Steavenson, Guy, Porter, Parker, Caulker, Bendal, and Atkinson ;
Who, with sundry other inhabitants, Military and
Militia, to the number of 123 persons, were, by
the tyrannic violence of Suraj-ud-dowlah,
Suba of Bengal,
Suffocated in the Black Hole Prison of Fort William,
on the night of the 20th day of June 1756,
and promiscuously thrown the suc-
ceeding morning into the Ditch
of the revelin of this place.
This monument is erected by their surviving fellow
sufferer,
J. Z. Holwell.
This horrid act of violence was as amply as deservedly
revenged on Suraj-ud-Dowlah, by his Majesty's
arms, under the conduct of Vice-Admiral
Watson and Colonel Clive, Anno 1757.

The east gate of the present Custom House represents the main gate of the old Fort; you drove straight to it from

Lall Bazar by the north of Dalhousie Square, having the garden on your left, and Writter's Buildings on your right. The monument stood in the middle of the road opposite to the Fort Gate, nearly where an ornamental lamp post has now been placed. The monument occupied the burial place of the 123 dead, which the inscription said were promiscuously thrown into the ditch of the ravelin of this place. The nearest approach to the site of the Black-Hole is the northern end of the eastern verandah of the new Post Office. Here the outer wall, of enormous strength, of the old Fort was standing in 1856.

The following extracts from a series of papers published in the "Englishman" Newspaper on the Tragedy of the Black-Hole, and particularly describing its site and surroundings, will be read with interest. They are from the pen of Dr. Busteed, of the Calcutta Mint.

"What the inner construction of the Fort was may be guessed at by any one entering a gate to the north of the Post Office and walking down, after a turn to his left, towards the river; on his right he will see what at first glance seems to be a double row of arches supported on short powerful and shapely columns, and facing him a portion of a broken wall, on which, and apparently on some of the arches, stands a house, now, I believe, occupied by the Post Master.

"Until lately the jutting out wall showed its rugged fracture, but recently this end has been squared off with new bricks and it as well as the little columns and arches near have been plastered over, thus concealing the small, neat, original brick-work.

"The wall is what remains of the southern curtain of the Fort; it is about nine feet thick. The arches and columns constitute the 'piazza' of the old descriptions. They are still in perfect preservation; the arches are about ten feet wide, the columns about four feet in diameter. There are about a dozen of the arches remaining.

"When one enters the cloister-like area, it may be seen that the inner arches have been filled up, otherwise one could see through them into what was the interior of the Fort, *i.e.*, the court-yard and parade.

"The piazza as now seen on the south side is about twenty feet wide, and went in all probability round the Fort, as did a range of buildings used as godowns or warehouses, lying between the piazza and the outer wall, *i e.*, having very little air and light admitted into them through the piazza which looked into the central open space of the Fort. The depth of the warehouses, *i. e.*, from the curtain wall behind them to the piazza was about fourteen feet, and those that adjoined the eastern wall were used as barracks.

"'On each side of the eastern gate' says Orme, 'extended a range of chambers adjoining to the curtain, and before the chambers a veranda or open gallery; it was of arched masonry and intended to shelter the soldiers from the sun and rain, but, being low, almost totally obstructed the chambers behind them from the light and air.' These were the barracks which according to Holwell 'were open to the west by arches and a small parapet wall corresponding to the arches of the veranda without.'

"If this was the accommodation provided for the good, well behaved soldiers in those days, how did the troublesome refractory ones fare? The Black Hole prison was at the south end of those barracks, *i. e.*, it was cut off from them by a wall containing a door opening inwards, and was provided with two small barred windows which were made by bricking up, a portion of two of the series of arches which the Black Hole had in common with the rest of the barracks. At the end of it was the east end of the southern wall; at the back was the dead eastern wall; in front the all but occluded arches (barred), on the north the interposed partition wall containing the door, through which the unfortunate soldier was run in, to be placed in the stocks, when maddened perhaps to insubordination by the heat, the darkness and the mosquitoes, his constant companions in the barracks proper." * * * * *

"A very good idea of the Black Hole may be derived from a visit to an existing apartment in the ruins of the old fort, into the formation of which the remnant of the outer southern wall enters. This room is quite open on one side (the eastern) and quite closed on two, while in front of it is the western end of the remaining piazza. In width, that is, from the curtain to the pillar and arch, it shows the corresponding measurement of the Black Hole. In fact, if the open side were provided with a wall containing a door, and if the two arches in front (or rather the arch and a half which would be comprised in eighteen feet), were partly bricked up and furnished with barred openings, there would be as accurate a model as one could have of the Black Hole, bearing in mind that the actual prison adjoined the other (eastern) end of the southern curtain. The room in question is now occupied by an official said to be the Jemadar of the Post Office Syces." **

"What remains of the old fort must have witnessed many of the circumstances of the final struggle; it was very near to the last scene of all, and is therefore intimately associated with the memory of Holwell and his brave companions in devotion and adversity. The present generation in Calcutta signalizes its appreciation of all this by converting part of the stage of so much that is historical into out-houses for the post office carts, syces and their indefinable litter, and by putting up latrines on it.

"Our predecessors neglected the memory of the defenders of Calcutta; we—dishonor it." * * * * *

"It is unlikely that anything more than a languid, spasmodic curiosity could now be aroused about those old remains of a by-gone age, except in the minds of a few antiquarians. Were it otherwise a vigorous effort of respectful representation to Government might perhaps get them saved from desecration and preserved to the public, before they are either pulled down or made to disappear by being drawn into the construction of modern buildings. The piazza might be cleared out, and purified and opened up, so as to show its just construction and proportion, and its interior be suitably occupied. A fac-simile of the tablet of Holwell's mouument containing his own inscription and the names, &c., might be assigned a niche in it. This is but a crude suggestion; I have no doubt that, if the occasion were to be brought about, others more practicable and appropriate would be forthcoming from competent sources.

"Apart from the respect paid to the memory of the dead, and apart from the desire to take away a great reproach from the city, which some such measure would testify to, it would render available to the public and to strangers, what is, incomparably, the most interesting Historical Monument in India in connexion with the British."

The Old Fort and Warehouses adjoining occupied the

site on which now stands the Custom House and new Post Office. A portion of it was pulled down in 1819, to make way for the Custom House, and the remainder was removed in 1856 to make way for the new General Post Office. The masonry was of such strength that pick-axe and crow-bar were of no avail, and blasting by gunpowder had to be resorted to. A section of the old wall is still visible. It is enormously thick and strong. The old builders of India, like the Romans, preferred tiles to bricks for walls.

The walls of the old Fort extended to the site of the Port Commisioner's Office on the Strand, in digging the foundations for which walls of great strength were disclosed. Similar disclosures were made in digging the foundations for the new East Indian Railway offices at the corner of Fairlie Place.

The new *St. John's Church* was opened with great ceremony on Easter Sunday in 1787. The Governor and principal inhabitants *walked* in solemn procession from the Old Court House to the church. At the consecration they contributed Rs. 3943 towards the establishment of a Free School.

West of St. John's, in the premises now occupied by the Stamp and Stationary Office, was formerly the *Old Mint*, in which the Company coined its Rupees from 1791 to 1832. Previous to 1791, the coinage was executed by contract. The first money was coined in Calcutta in 1762.

Opinions differ as to the precise locality of *Old Government House.* In Upjohn's map 1792-3, the Government House and Council-House occupy the spot on which the present Government House stands. Before that it was probably where the Treasury Buildings now stand. Mrs. Hastings is said to have lived in Hasting's Street, in the house now occupied by Messrs. Burn & Co.

In *Old Post Office* Street, was the Post Office, in a house nearly opposite to the High Court.

The *Town Hall* occupies the site of a house in which Mr. Justice Hyde lived, and for which he paid Rs. 1200 per mensem.

The *Supreme Court* was established in 1774; its sittings were first held in the Old Court House, which was pulled down in 1792. It was then removed to its present situation on the Esplanade Row, west.

The *Esplanade* formed a favourite promenade "of elegant walking parties" in moonlight-evenings. The five principal streets of Calcutta abutted on it. To the south was the *Maidan*, then covered with jungle, while "the course" led the ladies down to see an occasional launch at Watson's works at Kidderpore.

The *Respondentia Walk* extended a little below Baboo's Ghat. It was the resort of those fond of moonlight rambles, and of children, with their train of servants. Its position was no doubt indicated by the row of fine trees which stood south of Baboo's Ghaut, but most of which were destroyed in the Cyclone of 1864.

The *Strand Road* was formerly a low, sedgy bank, and the river near it was shallow, the deep channel being on the Howrah side; but owing to the formation of the Sumatra sand (so called from a ship of that name sunk there) the deep channel was thrown to the Calcutta side. The Strand Road was formed in 1823, from the funds of the Lottery Committee.

Baboo's Ghât was named from Raj Chandra Mir, who built it.

Close adjoining is *Chandpal Ghât.* "This is the post where India welcomes and bids adieu to her rulers. It is here that the Governors-General, the Commanders-in-Chief, the Judges of the High Court, the Bishops, and all who are entitled to the honors of a salute from the ramparts of Fort William, first set foot in the Metropolis. To enumerate all who have landed at these stairs, would be to recount the most distinguished men of the last seventy years. It is not noticed in the Map of 1756;—but we know that it was in existence in 1774, when Francis and his companions landed here, having had their sweet tempers soured by a five days' voyage from Kedgeree. It was here that the author of "Junius" counted one by one the guns which boomed from the Fort, and found to his mortification that they did not exceed seventeen, when he had expected nineteen. This circumstance appears to have laid the foundation for the implacable hatred which he manifested towards Hastings, and which for six years exposed the administration of the country to contempt. Is it unreasonable to suppose that if his self-esteem had been gratified by two additional charges of powder, the unseemly and dangerous opposition, which brought the empire to the brink of ruin, might have been avoided, and that even the solemn trial at Westminster Hall, so memorable for the rank of the victim, and for the splendid genius of his accusers, would never have taken place? Upon what trifles do the most momentous affairs of mankind appear to hang! And it was at this Chandpal Ghât that the first Judges of the late Supreme Court, who came out to redress the wrongs of India, but created infinitely more mischief than they remedied, first set foot in India. It was here that the Chief Justice, as he contemplated the bare legs and feet of the multitude who crowded to witness their advent, exclaimed to his colleague, 'See, brother, the wretched victims of tyranny. The Crown Court was not surely established before it was needed. I trust it will not have been in operation six months before we shall see all these poor creatures comfortably clothed in shoes and stockings'."*

The old Ghât has been recently removed to make way for the new embankment and the Port Commissioner's railway. A landing stage has been erected a few yards further north.

Proceeding north, we come to *Colvin's Ghât* formerly called the *Kutcha Goodee* ghât, or the place for collecting native boats. They were hauled upon the banks of the narrow creek before alluded to which ran through the town from this point to the Salt Water Lakes. It was on the banks of this creek, on the spot now occupied by the Bengal Secretariat, that the southern battery was thrown up in 1756.

In the immediate vicinity is the *Police Ghât*, and there, in ancient times, before the capture of Calcutta, stood the house and grounds of the President. The garden appears to have extended from the river to Tank Square, then the great resort of the community for recreation. After the capture of Calcutta, old Government House was turned into a "Bankshall" or Marine yard, and, at the ghât in front of it, a dock-yard was constructed in 1790 for the repairs of pilot vessels, which was disused and filled up in 1808.

* From "Notes on the left bank of the Hooghly" in Calcutta Review, Vol. III. 1845.

The next ghât was the *Old Fort Ghât*, and just above stands the *Bonded Warehouse* on the site of which stood the noble mansion of Mr. Cruttenden, subsequently the Governor of Calcutta, which was burnt down on the second night of the siege in 1756.

Immediately above it is Clive Street Ghât, which was known at the close of the last century as Blyth's Ghât, when that gentleman's large ship-building establishment was in its vigor.

Clive Street was, as now, the grand centre of business. Near where the Oriental Bank is now was the residence of Lord Clive.

Proceeding north, past the new Mint, we pass many Ghâts of little or no note until we arrive at the Baug Bazar Ghât, which formerly bore the name of Roghoo Mitter's Ghât after the son of Govindram Mitter, one of the most wealthy and influential natives of Calcutta, one hundred years ago.

Further north commences the *Chitpore road*,—a road which remains materially unaltered after the lapse of more than a century.* It received its name from the goddess *Chiteswari* who had a splendid temple here, erected by Govindram Mitter, where human sacrifices were formerly offered. The lofty dome of this temple fell with a crash, some fifty years ago, and it is now in ruins. Chitpore Road forms a continuation of the Dum-Dum Road, and was the old line of communication between Murshidabad and Kalighat.

---

* The introduction of the Tramway into Chitpore road, and the consequent increase of traffic, has rendered the widening of the street imperative, which is about to be carried out.

At this point the *Circular Canal* falls into the Hooghly. A large new lock and tidal basin has been constructed at the mouth of the Canal. The Canal is crossed by a suspension bridge, and a little beyond is the village of *Chitpore*, which appears from an ancient Bengallee poem, to have been in existence 300 years ago. Here was the residence of the Chitpore Nawab.

East of the Circular Road, is *Halsi Baghan*, formerly the garden-house of Omichand, [Amin Chand] "the Rothschild of his day,"—the great millionaire who, by his influence, could sway the court of Murshidabad. During forty years he was the chief contractor for providing the Company's investments, and realised more than a crore of rupees. He lived in this place with more than regal magnificence, and most of the best houses of Calcutta belonged to him. Omichand stipulated with the English for a reward of thirty lakhs for betraying Siraj-ud-Dowlah, but on finding that he was deceived by a fictitious treaty he lost his reason.

It was at this garden-house that Meer Madan, Siraj-ud-Dowlah's general, took up his head-quarters the day after Calcutta was captured, and it was hither that Mr. Holwell and two other European gentlemen were conveyed, with a burning fever in their veins, and thrust into a tent four feet long, three feet wide, and three feet high, where they remained during the night exposed to the rain, which fell in torrents, with only one-half their bodies protected by the canvas. But they had passed the previous night in the Black Hole, and the tent was paradise.

Baitakkkhanna Street, [Baithak-Khúnah] leading from Lall and Bow-Bazars to the Circular Road, received its name from the famous old tree which stood there and formed a "Baitakkhanna," or resting place for the merchants who traded to Calcutta, and whose caravans rested under its shade. "Here the merchants met to depart in bodies from Calcutta, to protect each other from robbers in the neighbouring jungle, and here they dispersed when they arrived at Calcutta with merchandise for the factory." Job Charnock is said to have chosen the site of Calcutta for a city, in consequence of the pleasure he found in sitting and smoking under the shade of a large tree. This tree is probably the Baitakkhanna tree which was standing in 1780. We read in Hickey's Gazette of "a Garden-house situate at Bread and Cheese Bungalo, opposite the great tree, and forms the angle of the two roads." In the same year Mr. Henry Cowen set up a school at the "Bread and Cheese Bungalo or Boytacannah."

Sealdah is described in 1757 as a "narrow causeway several feet above the level of the country, leading from the east." It was the scene of hard fighting in that year.

East of the Circular Road are the *Salt Water Lakes*,—a great tract of low country, regularly overflowed by the tide. They were formerly much nearer Calcutta than at present, that is to say, reclamation and natural silting are constantly diminishing their extent.

The following stray notes respecting the streets of Calcutta about the year 1780, will conclude this paper.

The space between Middleton Street, Theatre Road, and up to the Lower Circular Road, was called *Dihe Birjee*, from which the Birjee Tank, south of the Cathedral, got its name. *Loudon Street* recalls the name of the Countess of Moira and Loudon, in whose time it was built. *Russell*

Street after Sir H. Russell, Chief Justice, who built the first house there (now occupied as a boarding establishment.) *Free School Street* did not then exist. It was a jungle of bamboos, which people were afraid to pass at night. The old name of *Sudder Street* was *Ford Street.* The tank before it was called *Colinga Tank.* There was a street called Ahmud Jemadar's Street, where now Royd Street and Elliot's Road are. Many of the lanes about Cossitollah (now Bentinck Street) and Dalhousie Square, had the same names as at the present day, as Grant's, Weston's, Zig-zag, Imambari, Sooterkin's, Chandney Choke, Cooper's, Mangoe, Dacre's, Crooked, Fancy, and Larkin's Lane; also Raneemoody Gully (now British Indian Street, in compliment to the British Indian Association, which has its offices there.) A street rejoicing in the name of Corkscrew Lane, was situated north of Government house. It led from Merler Place to Fancy Lane. Along the Strand, where now the Bank of Bengal stands, was a road called King's Bench Walk, which led to Hasting's Street.

Many of the streets in the native quarters are called after things which were sold on the site of the existing streets; as *Suriparah* (wine sold), *Harikatta* (bones for combs), *Kolutola* (oil), *Chutturparah* (the place of Carpenters), *Chunam Gully* (lime) *Molunga* (salt), *Aheeritola* (cowherd's quarter) *Kumartola* (potter's tank). In many others, the names of old native proprietors are re-called.

But it is remarkable that there is not a single street which perpetuates the name of the founder of Calcutta, Job Charnock.

CALCUTTA IN THE PRESENT DAY.

CALCUTTA, the chief city of Bengal, the seat of the Supreme Government, and the Metropolis of India, stands in Lat. 22° 33′ N., and Long. 88° 23′ E. It is situated about 100 miles from the sea on the left bank of the western branch of the Ganges, called by Europeans the *Hooghly*, by natives *Bhagiratti*, and the true Ganges, and considered by them as a holy stream. The width of the Hooghly at Armenian Ghat is about 600 yards, but at other parts it widens to nearly a mile. Calcutta occupies a space along the bank of the river of about 4½ miles, estimated from Chitpore on the north, to Kidderpore on the south, and with an average width of a mile and a half from east to west, that is, from the river bank to the Circular Road, which forms the eastern boundary. Beyond which to the east and south-east are the suburbs of *Narkuldangah*, *Simlah*, *Sealdah*, *Entally*, *Ballygunge*, *Bhowanipore*, *Alipore*, *and Kidderpore*. The area of Calcutta is about seven square miles. The length of roads in the town is about 120 miles.

The ground on which Calcutta is built is a part of the alluvial deposits of the Gangetic delta, and is elevated not more than 16 or 18 feet above the mean sea level. The main stream of the Ganges has long since deserted this part of its delta, and now reaches the sea through the *Hurrin-*

H

gotta and the *Megna*, far to the eastward. But, according to native tradition, the *Hooghly*, or (under its native name) the *Bhagiratti*, was once the sacred stream, and an old temple which, till a few years ago, stood near the tank to the south of the Jail, and was believed to be 600 years old, is said to have been built on the bank of the Ganges, which at that time followed the line of Tolly's Nullah past Kalighat.

Excavations that have been made for tanks, foundations, &c., shew that to a depth of about 40 feet the surface formation is an alternation of sand and clay beds. A band of vegetable matter, which appears to indicate an old land surface, is met with at about 20 feet, (and therefore below the actual level of the sea), and from this down to 30 feet the stumps of *Soondri* trees, with their roots attached in the position of their growth, are frequently found; all of which indicate that the site of Calcutta was once occupied by marshy islands, flooded by the tides, and in the condition of the outer Sunderbuns of the present day; and that, since that time, the old land surface has sunk some 18 or 20 feet, and has been afterwards covered and raised by silt gradually deposited from the river waters.

At a depth of about 40 feet a bed of semi-fluid quicksand is met with; the existence of which renders it difficult to erect heavy and massive piles of building in Calcutta, and to preserve them vertical and without cracking. Indeed, many of the large buildings lately erected have suffered more or less by unequal sinking; especially the High Court building, and that of the new Museum in Chowringhee.

The general slope of the ground surface is very small, and, as is usually the case in river deltas, it is away from the river bank. The natural drainage of the land therefore tends towards the Salt Lake, and not into the Hooghly; and the admirable system of artificial drainage designed by Mr. W. Clark follows the same direction.

Being situated almost at the limits of the torrid zone, and within a degree of the tropic of cancer, the climate of the places is less uniform than that of Madras and other places nearer the equator. At the same time, owing to its maritime position, Calcutta is far from presenting those strong contrasts of season that are felt by residents of the N. W. Provinces, and generally in the interior. Three seasons may be distinguished, namely,—the hot season, lasting from the middle of March to the setting in of the rains in June; the rains, which usually set in in June and last till the end of September, or, in favorable years, to the middle or latter part of October, and the cold season from November to the early part of March. The average temperature of the whole year is 79·4°, that of the hot weather months 84·5° (of May 86°); that of the rains 83·3°, and that of the cold weather 71·5°. The highest temperature, 106° in the shade, has been recorded twice in the last twenty years, namely, in May 1867 and 1873, and the lowest temperature recorded by a thermometer exposed under a thatched shade is 51·4, namely, in January 1874. In the hot weather, when the wind is chiefly from the west and south-west, and sometimes heated to a temperature of 100° and upwards, Calcutta enjoys an advantage over stations more in the interior, in the sea breeze, which, as a rule, sets in late in the afternoon and blows for some hours after sunset. The intensity of the heat at this season is also mitigated by the occasional occurrence of a north-wester, a storm which, as its name imports, comes up from the west or north-west, more frequently than from any other direction, and is preceded by violent gusts of wind and clouds of dust, blowing outwards in advance of the storm. The lightning in these storms is sometimes very vivid, and a season rarely passes in which several houses are not struck by the electric discharge.

Most of the larger houses and public buildings are furnished with lightning rods, but they are very ineffective, and frequently afford proof that they have been put up simply in obedience to custom, and with but little comprehension of their use and action.

The average annual rainfall of Calcutta is 66 inches.* The greater part of this falls between June and October, during which time the temperature varies not more than about 8° during the twenty-four hours; the air is very damp, and rain is heavy and frequent, but not continuous. Clothes and books become mouldy if not frequently opened out and aired; and the heat, though less intense than in April and May, is more oppressive, producing a feeling of lassitude, which is very inimical to mental and bodily activity. To Europeans the latter part of the rains is the most unhealthy season of the year. It is at the beginning and close of the rainy season, namely, in May and June, and again in October and the early part of November, that Calcutta is most frequently visited by cyclones. These destructive storms always originate over the Bay of Bengal, sometimes as far down as the Nicobars and Andaman Islands; and after gathering strength for two or three days, with but little change of place, they move forward in a direction between north

* The highest on record, that of 1871, was 93·31 inches; the lowest that of 1837, was 43·61 inches; and the heaviest recorded fall, that of the 11th May 1835, was 12 inches in three hours.

and west, becoming fiercer and more destructive as they advance. The nature of these storms is now well understood. The winds blow spirally round and into a central region (the eye of the storm) where a perfect calm prevails, surrounded by winds of the greatest violence. When the centre of such a storm passes over any place the wind blows steadily from the same quarter (in Calcutta from the East or E. N. E.,) with increasing violence, until the central calm reaches it. There is then a complete calm, which lasts from a few minutes to an hour or more; and this is followed by a sudden renewal of the storm, with its maximum violence, from the opposite quarter of the compass. Calcutta has not been traversed by the centre of one of these storms since the 3rd June 1842;* but the storm of the 5th October 1864, when the centre passed a few miles to the west of the city, was not less destructive, the whole shipping of the river being carried away from its moorings, and a great part wrecked and stranded. Since its occurrence, a system of storm signals has been established for the information of the shipping, and whenever the weather appears threatening these are exhibited, both in Calcutta, and at three stations on the river below.

The conventional divisions of the city are two—*Northern* and *Southern*—Bow Bazar Street, continued in a line from the Circular Road to the river, forming the boundary. The Northern portion, with the exception of the business portion to the north-west of Dalhousie Square, is almost exclusively occupied by natives. The streets, like those of

* Described by the late Mr. H. Piddington in his Seventh Memoir on the Law of Storms. Journal As. Soc. Bengal, vol. xi.

most oriental towns, are narrow, and in some parts, the houses are lofty. A large portion of the northern area is occupied by bustees or native villages, covered with mud or straw huts, placed on the bare damp ground crammed together without ventilation or drainage, often grouped round a tank or pond which receives all the filth, and is at the same time used for washing if not for cooking purposes. The houses of the better classes are brick-built, from two to three stories high, and flat roofed. Those of the wealthier Baboos are usually built in the form of a hollow square, (many of the larger ones consist of a double quadrangle) which, on the occasion of Hindu festivals, is covered in and lighted up. On the northern side is the Thakoor-ghur, where the presiding deity is placed. The upper floor contains the living apartments, with verandahs, always inwards. Many of the older houses have also wooden verandahs or balconies facing the street. There are a few really fine mansions belonging to wealthy native gentlemen, but as a rule the native architecture presents a mean and dilapidated appearance.

The principal streets and squares in the Northern Division (running north and south) are the *Strand Road*, *Chitpore Road*, *College Street*, with its fine square and tank, round which are grouped the principal Educational Institions of the City; *Cornwallis Street*, also with a fine square and tank, one side of which is occupied by the General Assembly's Institution; and *Amherst Street*, the seat of the Church Missionary Institution, the Alms House, &c. Running east and west are *Baitakkhannah*; *Colootollah*, with its new westerly continuation called *Canning Street*; *Mochooa Bazar*, a fine though narrow street, continued to the east towards the Gas Works, and extended to the river under the name of *Cotton Street*, the abode of native merchants from Western India; *Beadon Street*, a new street recently constructed, leading from Nimtollah Street to the Circular Road, with a fine square about its centre; and also new *Grey Street*, a continuation of *Sobha Bazar Street*—one of the oldest streets in Calcutta,—extending to Circular Road.

The principal *Bazars* in the Northern Division are the *Radha Bazar*, the *Old* and *New China Bazar*, and the *Burra Bazar*. In the two former, liquors, oilman's stores, furniture, clothing, and an immense variety of other goods may be obtained at moderate prices, provided the purchaser has all his wits about him, and remembers that there is always what is called an "asking price," which is generally from one to two-thirds in excess of the price that will be taken.

In the Burra Bazar will be found, piece goods, Cashmere shawls, jewellery, precious stones, and hardware of every description. The visitor will hardly know whether to wonder most at the large stocks of goods which he may inspect, or at the wonderful dens in which they are stowed away.

The business part of the city, that is to say, the European portion of it, is mainly centred in *Dalhousie Square*, and the streets which branch from it and surround it. Speaking generally, the west portion is chiefly occupied by the merchants, and the south-east by tradesmen The principal shops—and there are some very fine ones—are to be found in the Square, in Old Court House Street, and in Government Place.

The Southern Division—between Bow Bazar and Dhurrumtollah—bounded on the west by Bentinck Street, is a district inhabited chiefly by East Indians, Portuguese, and Europeans of the lowest class, together with a considerable number of natives, which presents features as unpleasant as any part of Calcutta. Full of tortuous and narrow lanes, badly drained, and reeking with foul odours, thickly populated, and miserably housed, nothing but grinding poverty could induce Christian men to take up their abode in such a locality. In this district, on the north side of Dhurrumtollah, is the Bazar called "*Chandney Chouk,*" a labyrinth of filthy passages, lined with shops, in which may be found a wonderful collection of sundries, from a door nail to a silk dress.

South of Dhurrumtollah, commencing at Bentinck Street runs the noble *Chowringhee Road*, nearly two miles long and eighty feet broad. The eastern side is lined by handsome houses, each standing in its own compound or garden, and facing the fine *Maidan* which lies between them and the river. They are generally ornamented with spacious verandahs to the south, that being the quarter from which, in the hot weather, the cool evening breeze blows. Most of the houses are three stories high, and the rooms are spacious and lofty. All the out offices are detached from the house.

Parallel with Chowringhee Road runs *Wellesley Street*, which is continued in almost a straight line—a fine broad street—through *Wellesley Square*, the north side of which is occupied by the *Madrissa*, and *Wellington Square* which contains the Great Reservoir and the Pumping Station of the New Water Works, until it reaches the Circular

Road at the extreme north of the Town. To the east of Wellesley Street, and bounded on the north by Dhurrumtollah, on the south by Collinga, and on the east by the Circular Road, is the district called *Toltollah*, chiefly occupied by Mahomedan khalassies and lascars. *Park Street*, and the districts to the south of it, are almost entirely inhabited by Europeans, and contain some of the best residences in the city. Within the last fifteen years this quarter has been considerably extended, a large number of new houses having been erected, and new streets and squares formed, on sites formerly occupied by native bustees. There are also some good houses in the Circular Road, which has been drained and greatly improved by the construction of foot-paths, and the planting of avenues of trees.

The great *Maidan*, or plain, presents a most refreshing appearance to the eye, the heavy night dews, even in the hot season, keeping the grass green. Most of the fine trees with which it was studded were blown down in the cyclone of 1864. A few groups have been planted to replace them, and most of the maidan roads are now lined with young trees, which, if spared by future storms, will give a new aspect of beauty to the scene. On the maidan are several fine tanks, from which the inhabitants formerly obtained their water supply.

The following streets are identified with eminent names :—

Amherst Street, is called after Lord Amherst, Governor-General in 1823.

Baretto's Lane, after Joseph Baretto, a charitable Portuguese merchant, who died in 1824, bequeathing the munificent sum of five lakhs of Rupees for the benefit of various religious and charitable institutions.

Camac Street, named after William Camac, a gentleman who owned a laarge number of houses in that locality in the last century.

Elliot's Road, after John Elliot of the Bengal Civil Service, who, as President of the Boards of Police and Conservancy in Calcutta, "effected greater reforms in the city than any of his successors have done."

Esplanade Row, East, No. 9, now occupied by Messrs. T. E. Thomson and Co., was once the Residence of Warren Hastings, and No. 4, the Residence attached to R. Scott Thomson and Co., was formerly used as a Council Chamber, and until recently, an autograph of Warren Hastings was to be seen scratched on a pane of glass of one of the rooms.

Hare Street, after David Hare, a philanthropic Scotch watchmaker, who spent his life in laboring for the diffusion of high class education among the native community.

Loudon Street, recalls the name of the Countess of Moira and Loudon, in whose time it was built.

Kyd Street, after Colonel Kyd, best known as a distinguished Botanist, who was mainly instrumental in establishing the Calcutta Botanical Gardens in 1787.

Rawdon Street, after Lady Hastings, who was also Countess of Rawdon.

Royd Street, after Sir John Royd, one of the Judges of the late Supreme Court, who died in 1817.

Russell Street, after Sir James Russell, Chief Justice, who built the first house there.

THE SUBURBS.

The Suburbs of Calcutta environ the city on the north, east, and south sides of the Circular Road, the remaining boundary being formed by the River Hooghly. The Suburbs include the greater number of the *Punchannogram*, or the 55 villages purchased by the H. E. I. Company in 1717, and are within the Magisterial and Revenue Jurisdictions of the Twenty-four Pergunnahs. They comprise an area of 23 square miles.

At the extreme north is the village of *Cossipore* (Kasipur) where are the Government Gun Foundry, the Snider and Rifle Shell Factories—originally constructed by Col. Hutchinson, of the Engineers, after he had ransacked England and Europe for the best models. Now-a-days, however, but few guns are cast there. Here are also extensive Sugar Mills, and Jute Screw Houses. The Cossipore reach is one of the finest in the river, and is lined by a number of handsome villa residences, the property of the Seal family.

North of Cossipore, is "*The Seven Tanks*"—the well-known villa of the late Baboo Shama Churn Mullick. The house is a handsome and commodious structure, is splendidly furnished in European style, and contains a valuable collection of paintings and statuary. It is surrounded by an artificial canal expanding into a splendid tank in front, and crossed at intervals by bridges. The grounds are beautifully laid out. Adjoining is a handsome villa belonging to the Seal family, and, at no great distance, the *Paikpara Rajbari*, the family house of the sons of the late Protab Chunder Singh, to whom also belongs *Belgatchea Villa*, once well-known to the inhabitants of Calutta as the property of Dwarkanath Tagore, which contains many fine works of Art. The grounds are extensive and well laid out. There is also the residence of the late *Raja Buddynauth Rai*, where was formerly a fine Menagerie, all now in ruins.

To the south, is the village of *Chitpore* which appears to have been in existence 300 years ago. It was then written Chittrupoor, and was noted for the temple of Chittru, or Kalee, renowned for the number of human sacrifices formerly offered at her shrine. Here were the house and garden of the Chitpore Nawab, Mahomed Reja Khan, to whom the whole administration of Bengal was entrusted for several years after the Company had obtained the Dewanee.

Crossing Chitpore Bridge, and passing southwards through a district almost entirely inhabited by natives, we come to *Narkaldungah* where are the extensive works of the Oriental Gas Company.

Sealdah comes next, in which are the Termini of the Eastern Bengal, and the Calcutta and South Eastern Railways—the former a handsome and commodious structure. There are also several Jute Screws and the offices and depôts of the Labor Transport Company and other Emigration Agencies. The European population is very small. Here also is the Pauper Hospital,—now called the "Campbell Medical School."

Proceeding south, is *Entally*, an extensive district intersected with numerous tortuous roads and lanes. It contains a large number of European residences, some of them fine buildings in extensive grounds. Pleasant enough during the cold season, there is too much jungle to make Entally a healthy residence in the rains, or even in the hot weather. Here are the Municipal Foundry and Workshops, the Municipal Slaughter houses and the Pumping Station of the Drainage Works, where the whole sewage of the city is pumped into a high level sewer and conveyed to the Salt Water Lakes, where an open channel conveys it to within reach of tidal influence. The Municipal Railway runs by the side of the sewer and conveys some 250 tons of sweepings daily which are employed to raise a square mile of land which has been bunded off from the lakes for the purpose. South of Entally is the fine Volunteer Rifle Range, constructed in 1877.

Ballygunge.—Here there is a fine open maidan, adjoining which are the Barracks and Exercise Ground of the Governor-General's Body Guard. Around this maidan, and lining some of the adjoining roads, are many very fine European residences standing in extensive grounds, and presenting great attractions to those who are kept by business during the day in the hot and dusty town. But unfortunately a heavy penalty has often to be paid during the rains in the shape of fever, which is found to be exceedingly difficult to shake off.

Bhowanipore is a populous native place, inhabited chiefly by Hindu artizans in metals who work for the houses in town. The London Missionary Society's Institution is in Bhowanipore, and also the Lunatic Asylum. Bhowanipore is on the road to Kalighat, the great Hindu temple—great not from any structural beauty, but as the shrine at which all good Hindus worship when they leave their own "Thakoor

Bari." There is a constant stream of traffic to and fro. Kali-ghat is thickly populated; the principal houses belong to the Haldars, the priestly family attached to the temples. The present temples were erected by the Chowdry family in 1809. Beyond is *Tollygunge*, a station of the Church Missionary Society, near which is a group of handsome Hindu temples erected in 1796 by Ram Nath Mundul. Beyond is *Russapugla*, the residence of the Mysore family—the descendants of Tippoo Sultan.

To the eastward of Bhowanipore, crossing the Tolly's Nullah, we come to *Alipore*, the residence of the Lieutenant-Governor of Bengal, the Head Quarters of the "Presidency Division" and of the 24-Pergunnahs, and also a Military station for a native regiment. Here also are the great Jail of the District, the Army Clothing Agency, the General and Military Offices, the Government Telegraph Store Yards and Workshop. In the last century, Warren Hastings had his favorite villa at Alipore, which still bears his name. There are many beautiful residences in this locality, and its reputation for healthiness is good. A tract of land on the banks of Tolly's Nullah formerly thickly covered with huts, has recently been cleared, and laid out, at the cost of Government, as a *Zoological Garden*.

Kidderpore is extensively populated, principally by natives. Here are the Military Orphan School, a Church, and Schools, the Mazzuchelli Bazar, and the Government Dockyard.

Nearer the river is *Hastings*, formerly "Coolie Bazar,"—a Government colony, consisting chiefly of warrant officers and conductors connected with the Ordnance and Commissariat Departments. Here also are the Commissariat Godowns.

Crossing the Hastings Bridge, we arrive at *Garden Reach*, the oldest and best known suburb. The river bank for a distance of two miles, is lined by beautiful houses standing in large compounds, erected between the years 1768 and 1780, formerly the residences of the *élite* of the Metropolis; but now, and for some years past, less frequented, partly on account of the settlement of the ex-King of Oudh and his swarm of followers in the finest part of this beautiful suburb. The well-known residence of Sir Lawrence Peel, with its beautiful Garden, at Matiabrooz, the extreme south of the Reach, was first assigned to the Royal Captive; gradually fourteen fine houses have been purchased and occupied, and jealously surrounded by lines of high walls. The ex-King has a fine collection of Beasts, Birds, and Snakes.

Higher up the Reach are the premises and Landing Jetties of the *Messageries Maritimes;* and still higher the premises of the *Peninsular and Oriental Steam Navigation Company*, which consisted formerly of eight large upper-roomed houses, besides large workshops and stores. Since the transfer of the principal part of the Company's Establishment to Bombay, these have been mostly vacated. The Agent's residence is a handsome structure, erected after a design by Mr. C. K. Robinson, to whose architectural taste the city is indebted for some of its noblest buildings.

Still further north are the premises of the *India General Steam Navigation Company.*

THE STRAND ROAD.

From Hastings Bridge, a fine broad road extends north along the banks of the river, forming the evening promenade.

PRINSEP'S GHAT.

Just above Hastings, under the south-west angle of the fort, is a handsome structure in the Grecian Ionic style of architecture. It was erected by the citizens of Calcutta to perpetuate the memory of JAMES PRINSEP, "one of the most eminent men of his day, who, after a short and brilliant career, fell a sacrifice to his ardor in the pursuits of science." Victor Jaquemont, in his Travels in India, from 1828 to 1832, writes thus of Mr. Prinsep:—"He devotes his mornings to architectural plans and drawings, his days to assaying at the Mint, and his evenings to musical concerts."

Immediately opposite the Water Gate of the Fort stands

THE GWALIOR MONUMENT.

It was erected by Lord Ellenborough, Governor-General of India in 1847, in memory of the officers and men who fell in the Gwalior Campaign of 1843. It was designed by Col. H. Goodwyn, Bengal Engineers.

The structure is built of brick, faced with Jeypore

marble, surmounted by a metal dome or cupola supported on columns manufactured by Messrs. Jessop & Co., of this city, from guns taken from the enemy. In the centre is a sarcophagus, on which are engraved the names of the officers and men who fell in the battles of Maharajpore and Panniar. The height is 58 feet 6 inches.

Baboo's Ghat

Is a handsome colonnade of the Grecian Doric order. It bears the following inscription :—

"The Right Hon'ble Lord William Cavendish Bentinck, Governor-General of India, with a view to encourage public munificence to works of public utility, has been pleased to determine that this Ghât, erected at the expense of Baboo Rajchunder Doss in 1838, shall hereafter be called Baboo Rajchunder Doss' Ghât."

Just above is the engine house and pumping machinery by which the city is supplied with water for street watering purposes.

Opposite Baboo's Ghât and immediately south of the Esplanade Road are

The Eden Gardens,

for which the inhabitants are indebted to the liberality and taste of the Misses Eden, sisters of Lord Auckland, Governor-General of India, whose statue stands in the gardens. Here is the Band stand, where the Town Band, or the Band of the European Regiment stationed in the Fort, discourse sweet music every evening. A large space is laid out and turfed as a promenade, at one end of which stands a fine marble statue of Sir William Peel, Commander of Her Majesty's Frigate *Shannon*, who led his crew with their guns up to the walls of Lucknow, during the Mutiny of 1857, and died there of small pox. The gardens are laid out with winding paths and artificial water, interspersed with a profusion of beautiful flowering trees and shrubs—a pleasanter place for a morning or evening stroll cannot be found. In the gardens is a fine BURMESE PAGODA, removed from Prome after the last war in 1854, and re-erected here in 1856. Adjoining the gardens is the ground of the

CALCUTTA CRICKET CLUB,

on the west side of which is a neat pavilion. Round the whole is a broad turfed ride for equestrians, enclosed by pleasant walks and plantations.

OUT-DOOR MONUMENTS AND PUBLIC STATUES.

In addition to those named there are several other statues on the maidan.

South of the Esplanade (East) stands the *Ochterlony Monument*, raised in honor of SIR DAVID OCHTERLONY, Resident in Malwa and Rajpootana in 1823, "for 50 years a soldier, he had served in every Indian War from the time of Hyder downwards." It is a fine column, 165 feet in height, with a Sarancenic capital. A splendid panoramic view of the city and neighbourhood is obtained from its summit.

Opposite the Town Hall is a bronze statue of LORD WILLIAM BENTINCK, Governor-General of India, 1828-1835, bearing the following inscription :—

"To William Cavendish Bentinck, who, during 17 years, ruled India with eminent prudence, integrity and benevolence: who, placed at the head of a great empire never laid aside the simplicity and moderation of a private citizen, who infused into Oriental Despotism the Spirit of British Freedom; who never forgot that the end of Government is the welfare of the governed; who abolished cruel rites; who effaced humiliating distinctions; WHO ALLOWED LIBERTY TO THE EXPRESSION OF PUBLIC OPINION; whose constant study it was to elevate the moral and intellectual character of the nation committed to his charge."

A little further west, and opposite the main entrance to the High Court is a full length statue of Lord Northbrooke, on a granite pedestal, bearing the following inscription on its four sides, in English, Bengali, Persian, and Hindi:—

"Thomas George, Earl of Northbrooke, Viceroy and Governor-General of India, 1872-76. Erected by public subscription."

At the South-west corner of the Government House grounds is a bronze equestrian statue of Lord Canning, Governor-General and first Viceroy of India. It was modelled by *J. H. Foley*,* R. A., and *T. Brock*, and stands on a handsome granite pedestal, and bearing the following inscription:—

"Charles John, Earl Canning, K.G., G.C.S.I., Governor-General and 1st Viceroy of India, 1856-62. Born 14th December, 1812. Died 17th June 1862."

Facing the south entrance to Government House is a full

* This was the last work upon which this celebrated sculptor was engaged. He died before it was completed, and the work was carried out by his pupil, Mr. Brock.

length bronze statue of LORD LAWRENCE, Viceroy and Governor-General of India, 1864-1869, executed by *J. Woolmer.* The statue stands upon a large and imposing base, and bears no inscription.

At the south-east of Government House, on a triangular plot called "The Cocked Hat," is a fine bronze-equestrian statue of LORD HARDINGE, Governor-General of India, 1844-1848. It was modelled by *J. H. Foley*, R. A., and is undoubtedly one of the masterpieces of this great sculptor. On the granite pedestal is the following inscription :—

"The Statue was erected by the inhabitants of British India of various races and creeds to HENRY VISCOUNT HARDINGE, in grateful commemoration of a Governor who, trained in war, sought by the acts of Peace to elevate and improve the various Nations committed to his charge, and when re-called to arms by unprovoked invasion at *Moodkee*, *Feroshuhur*, and *Sobraon*, maintained the reputation which, in youth, he won by turning the tide of victory at *Albuera.*"

In the centre of the Bentinck Road, at the point where it is crossed by the road leading from Jaun Bazar to Kidderpore, is placed a very fine bronze-equestrian statue to EARL MAYO, Viceroy of India, 1869-1870, bearing the following inscription :*—

"To the honoured and beloved memory of Richard Southwell, 6th EARL of MAYO, K.P., G.M.S.I. Humane, Courteous, Resolute and Enlightened, struck down in the midst of a Patriotic and Beneficent career on the 18th

* This statue was unveiled by H. R. H. the Prince of Wales on 31st December, 1875. It was first erected on the triangle south-east of Government House, and subsequently removed to its present site.

February, 1872, by the treacherous hand of an assassin, the People of INDIA, mourning and indignant, raise this Statue. Born, 21st February, 1822. Assumed the Viceroyalty, 12th January, 1869."

Opposite the entrance to Park Street is a bronze equestrian statue, by *Foley*, of SIR JAMES OUTRAM, which was unveiled with great ceremony by the Commander-in-Chief in 1874. It is raised on a lofty granite pedestal, which bears the following inscription :—

"SIR JAMES OUTRAM, Lieut-General, G. C. B., Baronet. His life was given to India : in early manhood he reclaimed wild Races by winning their hearts ; *Ghazni*, *Khelat*, the *Indian Caucasus*, witnessed the daring deeds of his prime ; *Persia* brought to sue for peace, *Lucknow* relieved, defended, and recovered, were fields of his later glories. Faithful servant of England, large-minded and kindly ruler of her subjects ; in all the True Knight ; 'The Bayard of the East.'

Born 29th January, 1803. Died 11th March 1863."

POPULATION.

An air of mystery long hung over the question of the population of Calcutta, numerically speaking, which one would think, on the face of it, might easily have been solved by a Census. Experience proved the contrary, for in spite of repeated enumerations until 1876 the number of the population was very uncertain. Let us notice the successive attempts which have been made:—

1752,	Mr. Holwell's estimate ...	409,000
1800,	By Police Committee ...	500,000
1814,	By Sir E. Hyde East ...	700,000
1821,	By Four Assessors ...	179,917
1821,	By Calcutta Magistrates ...	205,600
1831,	By Captain Steel, Superintendent of Police	410,930
1837,	By Captain F. W. Birch, Superintendent of Police ...	229,714
1850,	By Mr. Simms, Surveyor of Calcutta	361,369
1866,	By the Justices of the Peace ...	377,924
1872,	Ditto. ...	447,601
1876,	Ditto. ...	429,535

The Census has been again taken in April 1881, much greater care having been expended over the enumeration. The result shows the following total, *viz* :—

Town	...	... 433,219
Suburbs	...	... 251,439
	Total	... 684,658

The following is a Comparative Statement of the Town population, in 1876 and 1881:—

	Census of 1876.	Census of 1881.
Males	282,506	288,817
Females	147,029	144,402
Both Sexes	429,535	433,219
	1876.	1881.
Town Proper... ...	409,036	401,671
Fort William	2,803	3,348
Port	17,696	28,200
Total ...	429,535	433,219

The vast disproportion of the sexes is accounted for by the fact that although a large proportion of the natives, both Hindus and Mahomedans, are married men, a very large percentage of those resident in Calcutta are "grass-widowers." It may also be fairly presumed that, in a country where the females of all but the lowest classes are kept in a state of seclusion, a degree of unwillingness exists to make accurate returns which may go far to account for the disproportion of sexes alluded to.

The following principal Divisions are given:—

TOWN 1881.

Hindus ...	278,762	Jews	982
Mahomedans	124,430	Parsees	141
Christians ...	26,430	Sikhs	278
Brahmos ...	423	Others	52
Buddhists ...	1,721		

The following is the return for the Suburbs as shown in 1881:—

SUBURBS.

	Males.	Females.	Total.
Hindus ...	87,415	62,515	149,930
Mahomedans ...	57,121	39,462	96,583
Christians ...	2,019	2,029	4,048
Others ...	650	228	878
Total ...	147,205	104,234	251,439

In the Suburban Districts are included the inmates of the Alipore Central Jail, the Cantonments of Alipore and Ballygunge, and the several Emigration Depôts, as also the floating population on the River Hooghly and Canals.

There are 60 Schools and Patshallas in the Suburbs, affording education to 2,603 boys and 265 girls—a far from satisfactory average; but it must be borne in mind that many of the children of the middle and wealthy classes attend Educational Institutions within the town of Calcutta. Of the total male population one in every five persons can read and write, or are under instruction. Of the female population, only one in 37 is returned as able to read and write, or under instruction.

The *European Community* does not differ essentially in its composition from that of other large cities, excepting in the almost entire absence of the European Artizan, who forms so important an element in the population of English towns. The few British Mechanics in Calcutta are not actual laborers in their crafts at all, but merely supervisors of the work, which is almost entirely performed by natives. Of course the official element is very strong, and Law, Physic, and the other professions are well represented. Of Merchants there is, nominally, a goodly list; but a large proportion of them are more properly speaking Commission Agents. The Tradesmen, for extent and variety of stock, will compare favorably with the same class at home, and if the prices seem at first sight somewhat startling to the newly-arrived Londoner, it must be remembered that the Rupee with which payment is made is really worth only about *One and Eight Pence*, and that the expenses and risks of business in India are greatly in excess of those belonging to similar businesses in England.

The term *Eurasian* was invented by the late Marquis of Hastings, and is now applied to the progeny or descendants of European fathers and Hindu or Mahomedan mothers. They are not as a rule an active and energetic race; but there are not a few who have attained, and still hold, most deservedly, high official rank and positions of trust in Mercantile and other Offices.

The Portuguese of the present day are nearly allied in race to the natives, and are in fact Portuguese in little more than name. The first European conquerors in India, possessing in the sixteenth century the absolute command of the lucrative trade between the East and the West, without rival or control,—a century later this imposing fabric fell to ruin; one by one the Eastern possessions of Portugal were wrested from her; and the only territory she now possesses in India are Goa, Damân and Diû, with a population of about 500,000. A few, very few Merchants of this Nationality remain in Calcutta; but the bulk of those bearing Portuguese names, such as DeSouza, DeRozario, DeCosta, DeCruz, &c., are employed as Clerks, Printers, and even as Cooks, and many of the females as Ayahs or Nurse Maids.

The Armenians were among the earliest traders to India, coming from the Persian Gulf to Khorasan, and from thence by Kandahar and Kabul to Delhi, and thence to Benares, Patna, and Bengal.

About 250 years ago they formed a settlement at Sydabad (in the environs of Cossimbazar), and when the Dutch settled at Chinsurah in 1625, they were followed by the Armenians. The Armenian chiefs who joined the Dutch were of the Markar family from Shosh.* On the establishment of Calcutta in 1690, the Armenians accepted the invitation of Charnock and placed themselves under the protection of his Government. They participated with the English in the misfortunes of 1756, and received in compensation for their losses the sum of seven lakhs of Rupees. The Armenian community is a rich and thriving one.

---

* A stone in the Armenian Church at Chinsurah bears the following inscription:

"Here lies interred the famous Kharib *(i. e. foreigner)* Cojee Johannes, the son of Markar, an Armenian from Julpha, of the country of Shosh. He was a considerable merchant, honoured with the favours of kings and viceroys. He travelled North, South, East and West, and died at Hooghly in Hindoostan, November the 7th, 1697."

The Greeks. Commerce allured the Greeks, as well as the Armenians, to associate with the English in India. The first eminent Greek who settled in Calcutta was Hadjee Alexios Argyree, a native of Philippopolis: he came to Bengal in 1750. The Greeks of the present day are mostly successful Merchants.

The Parsees are the fewest in number, but inferior to none of the people of Calcutta in integrity, enterprise, and commercial skill.

The Jews are of course of various nationalities. Several of the best families come from Bagdad. They are extensive speculators in opium, and many of them have amassed great wealth.

The Chinese in Calcutta are chiefly of two classes,—Shoemakers and Carpenters. In both trades they are neat, expert, and industrious. They excel in ladies' and children's shoes. As carpenters, they are employed on boardship, and as pattern-makers in foundries. Many of them indulge largely in opium, and they are also much given to gambling. They are independent in their bearing, cheerful and obliging.

Of the *Native Population*, the bulk of course are natives of Bengal Proper—Hindus or Mahomedans.

The Hindus are separated into four great castes, or religious divisions—*Brahmins*, the first and most distinguished, to whom are entrusted the performance of religious ceremonies, the instruction of the people, and who alone are permitted to read the Vedas or sacred books; the *Chetris* of royal and military descent; the *Kaisyas*, merchants and cultivators; the *Sudras*, labourers and artificers. These four castes are split into an infinite number of subdivisions, differing in some matters of religion and domestic usage ; while a fifth great class, called *Pariahs*, or *Chandalls*, comprehends all who have violated some leading principle in the religion of the other four, and have therefore been banished from the society of the faithful ; and all who follow the lowest professions in the scale of Hindu society. The most important section in the third division is that of he *Kayasthas*, or writer caste, who number, according to the Census of 1872, 33,348 next comes the *Baniah* or grain-dealer, numbering 21,639. The *Brahmins* number 36,369.

The Mahomedans are mostly employed as Khitmatgars, Ayahs, Cooks, Coachmen, Syces, Derzies, Dufftries, Bhisties, Coolies, Raj-Mistrees (brick-layers), Painters, and a large number as Lascars, or sailors and boatmen. Some of the better educated hold respectable positions as Engineers and Draftsmen, Mooktears or Law Agents, and in the subordinate Medical Establishment.

Under this head, too, must be placed the *Arabs*, who are chiefly traders with the Persian and Arabian Gulf and Coasts, and one great item of their traffic lies in Arab horses. They own several large ships, which trade regularly to this port.

Next in importance, in point of number, are the Ooryahs—natives of Orissa, a steady, useful and hard-working race, employed chiefly, as Palkee bearers, House-servants, Punkah-pullers, Gardeners and Khalassies. Of these there are nearly 20,000 in Calcutta. Then there are the Mercantile classes—the *Marwarrees*, *Mahrattas*, *Goojerattees*, and others from Western India, dealers in opium, piece-goods, country produce, &c., shrewd men at a bargain, and not over-particular. The *Rajpoots* are high caste men, and are mostly employed as Durwans or door-keepers. They are generally trustworthy men, and they have need to be, as almost implicit trust is placed in them.

MUNICIPAL.

The constitution of the Calcutta Municipality is somewhat peculiar, if not unique. Previous to the year 1863, the affairs of the town were administered by Commissioners appointed by Government in 1848, who, in their first half-yearly Report, made a strong appeal to Government for funds to carry on their work. Among other funds they suggested that the Akbaree Tax, the Surplus Canal Tolls, the Ground Rent of Calcutta, and the balance at credit of the Court of Requests, amounting to about 4 lacs of rupees should be placed at their disposal. They write :—

"In order further to shew the necessity for some such increase of funds, the Committee consider they ought to state that the great improvements in Calcutta effected in past years were made not from the present assessment only, but from funds derived from the Government lotteries.

"These lotteries were conducted for a series of years under the auspices of Government, and the profits resulting from them were devoted to the improvement of Calcutta.

"The town is indebted to the Lottery Funds for the Strand Road, the Central Road, and numerous other great thoroughfares, as well as the public squares and tanks that now exist in many parts of it; and these are but a small portion of the improvements that have been effected with money derived from that source. Since its abolishment not only have no improvements of any note been made to the town, but the works of utility and ornament which executed from the profits of the lotteries are falling into decay from want of funds to keep them in repair."

It does not appear that their request was complied with, but some new powers of taxation were conferred, as, in 1852, the income of the Commissioners had risen to Rs 3,75,500; and in 1858, it had reached Rs 6,62,415.

The Commissioners did good work in their day, among which may be noticed the promotion of various important improvements in the Southern Division. A large bustee or native village which stood between Theatre Road and Circular Road, was purchased by some enterprising capitalists, and on the site a new square—Victoria Square—was laid out, with adjacent streets all now lined with new and handsome houses. Another bustee in Park Street was also removed and replaced by a triangular tank and garden. It was under the auspices of the Commissioners also that the great work of draining the city was commenced.

In 1855, Mr. William Clark, then a District Engineer on the East Indian Railway, was appointed Secretary and Engineer to the Commissioners.

In 1859 a contract was entered into with the Oriental Gas Company for lighting the City with gas; and on the 6th July of that year, Chowringhee was for the first time illuminated with gas, to the great wonderment of the natives, and to the satisfaction of the European community. The new system was gradually extended throughout the city, in which there are now 3,859 gas lamps.

Meanwhile Mr. Clark was preparing his grand scheme for the Drainage and Water Supply of Calcutta, which was submitted to a Scientific Committee, and, in 1859, the works were sanctioned by Government, and commenced—the estimates being for the Drainage Works, Rs 37,81,000; and for the Water Supply, Rs 28,00,000.

The whole of the drains are underground, and they are of various sizes from the main out fall brick sewer of 20 feet diameter, to the pipe drain of 6 inches. The main sewers are connected for flushing purposes with the river, whence they fall eastwards to the intercepting sewer on the Circular Road.

The sewage is pumped up at Palmer's Bridge, about a mile from the Circular Road, into a high level sewer, and discharged at a distance of about three miles into the Salt Water Lakes. The Pumping Station is well worth a visit.

The construction of Foot-paths has proceeded concurrently with the extension of the drainage works; and every drained street and lane which will admit of it, has now its raised causeway, of a width proportioned to the width of the street. This, with the filling up of the open drains, which ran on the side of almost every street, and the removal of the unsightly brick aqueducts through which the muddy river water was forced by the Chandpal Ghât engine, constitute the most striking features in the external improvement of Calcutta.

Those whose lot it was, twenty years ago, to grope their way through the slush and mire of the streets, dimly lighted as they then were with glimmering oil lamps, can best appreciate the change.

By an Act of the Bengal Council in 1863, a Municipality was constituted under the style of "The Justices of the Peace for the Town of Calcutta." The Justices 104 in number, were appointed by the Lieutenant-Governor of Bengal, about half being Europeans, and the rest natives and other nationalities, all classes being pretty fairly represented.

The Justices of the Peace carried out some good works of improvement, the most prominent of which are the Water Supply, the Drainage Works, the New Market, and the opening out of several New Streets and one Square in the northern or native division of the town.

In the course of 16 years they borrowed upwards of ₨ 1,50,00,000, or about a million and a half sterling, involving for interest and sinking fund a charge of more than ₨ 10,00,000 annually. To meet this heavy charge taxation was enormously increased.

For several years there was a good deal of friction between the independent European Justices, and Sir Richard Temple, the Lieutenant-Governor of Bengal, backed by the Chairman and the Native Justices. In 1876, finding it hopeless to do any further good, all the independent Justices resigned their offices, and no one being willing to take their places, it was necessary to form a new Municipal constitution, which came into existence as the "Calcutta Municipality" under an Act of the Bengal Council in 1876.

The present Municipality is partially elective, fifty "Commissioners" being elected by a portion of the rate-payers, and twenty-five being nominated by the Lieutenant-Governor of Bengal. It cannot be considered in any sense of the word *representative*. The Europeans and Eurasians as a class have held almost entirely aloof from it, either as voters or Commissioners, their representatives being only

4 out of 50 elected members. Great difficulty is experienced in inducing any independent Europeans to accept the Government nomination. The popular feeling amongst Europeans and Eurasians is, that any constitution which does not give them at least half the seats on the board cannot be satisfactory, since the town owes its existence and importance, almost solely to European capital and energy.

The principal officers of the Municipality are a Chairman, appointed by a Government (who is also the Commissioner of Police); and a Vice-Chairman, Engineer, Health Officer, and Secretary, appointed by the Commissioners.

The *New Water Supply* is the Justices' *Magnum Opus*. The water is pumped from the river Hooghly at Monerampore, about two miles north of Barrackpore, passed through filter beds, and brought down to Tallah by a 42-inch iron main, from whence it is distributed at a pressure of 50 feet. There is a large reservoir and pumping station at Wellington Square, which supplies the pressure to the Southern Division. The total length of water piping laid throughout the town is about 120 miles.

The works were constructed for a supply of six million of gallons daily, but they are actually supplying nearly 7½ million gallons; this has been found insufficient, and a supplemental supply of unfiltered river water has been provided, chiefly for street-watering, at a cost of Rs. 2,38,-244. The length of piping laid under this scheme is 25¼ miles.

The new Water Supply came into operation in May 1870, and the total cost of construction up to the end of 1880 has been a little more that 77 lakhs of Rupees. The expenditure for interest on capital and working expenses for 1880 was Rs. 4,72,060. It may be added that the analysis of the water shows that it is of exceptional purity.

The income of the Municipality for the year 1880 amounted to Rs 24,93,284, derived principally from house-rate, water-rate, lighting-rate, police rate, trades licenses, carriage, horse, and hackery licenses, &c, and the expenditure to Rs. 18,92,479.

In the year 1865 the Justices constructed a *Railway* from Bhag Bazar to a spot on the Circular Road, nearly opposite South Colinga Street, with a branch to the Salt Water Lakes, about 12 miles in length, at a cost of about 6½ lakhs. It is used partly for the conveyance of materials from the ghât, but principally for the removal of the street sweepings, of which 10,000 truck loads annually are conveyed to the Salt Lake, and there employed in the reclamation of a square mile of land, which has been "bunded" for the purpose.

In 1865, attention was drawn to the state of the Slaughter Houses in Entally, and a new one was constructed by the Justices, which has been worked with great success. The old slaughter houses have been suppressed.

The Municipal Market.

In conjunction with this, the establishment of a Market for the sale of all kinds of food for European consumption, was for years under consideration; and at last, in 1866, it was resolved to construct one on a large and complete scale, and the old bazar called Fenwick's bazar, with the filthy lanes and bustee surrounding, was taken up for the purpose. The market was opened in 1874. It is an extensive building, forming three sides of a quadrangle. The principal entrance is in Lindsay Street, to which it presents a frontage of about 300 feet. The property extends north to Jaun Bazar Street, (recently re-named Municipal Office Street) where the

NEW MUNICIPAL OFFICE

has been erected. It is a substantial and well-arranged building, and the improvement to this part of the town is very great. The land and market building cost about Rs 6,65,000. The Justices subsequently bought the Dhurrumtollah bazar for seven lakhs. The whole of this money was raised by Government loan, the interest of which is fully met by the rents of the stalls and shops in the market.

THE SUBURBAN MUNICIPALITY.

The Municipality for the Suburbs of Calcutta was called into being on the passing of the District Municipal Improvement Act (Act III of 1864, B. C.) under the Lieutenant-Governorship of Sir Cecil Beadon. Under the Act, the Magistrate of the district for the time being is *ex-officio* Chairman; and there is also a Vice-Chairman, who is the Executive Officer. The Members of the Municipality are appointed by the Lieutenant-Governor of Bengal, and are about 40 in number.

The chief sources of Revenue are House-rate, Horse and Carriage Tax, License Fees, &c., and the amount realised in the year 1874-75 was Rs 4,132,162. The Expenditure for the year was Rs 4,05,865.

The Municipality commenced its operations under serious difficulties. The great Cyclone of 1864 rendered hundreds of the poorer classes houseless and pauperised; the year 1866 was a year of general distress, while the Cyclone of 1867 again interfered most seriously with the collections. But the Municipality has struggled successfully through all troubles, and has accomplished a fair share of usefulness. It has no debt, and has a fair balance at its Bankers.

POLICE.

The expense of the Police of the City is provided for by a tax on householders, towards which Government contributes one-fourth. The post of Commissioner of Police is held by the Chairman of the Municipality. The force consists of 1 Deputy Commissioner; 4 European Superintendents; 27 European Inspectors; 10 European Town Serjeants; 40 European Constables; 9 Darogahs; 33 Serjeants; 36 Corporals; and 1,228 Constables. The total annual cost is about Rs. 4,28,000.

COMMISSIONERS FOR MAKING IMPROVEMENTS IN THE PORT OF CALCUTTA.

These Commissioners constitute the Calcutta Port Trust, a body incorporated under Act V., B. C., of 1870, for providing in the Port proper facilities for landing, shipping, and delivering goods, and for carrying out works of general improvement within the limits of the Port. Such a Trust for the Port of Calcutta was proposed so far back as 1862, but several years passed before any steps were taken in this direction, and in the meantime the Port of Calcutta had the reputation of being the dearest, and at the same time, as regards the provision of modern appliances to facilitate shipping business, the most backward port in the world.

To remedy this state of things an Act was passed in 1866, by which the Municipality was entrusted with the duties appertaining to a Port Trust, but for certain reasons this body proved unable to carry out the duty thus imposed upon it; and at the urgent solicitation of the Mercantile community, Government determined to constitute a separate body of Trustees to carry out this work of Port improvement. With this object the Act above referred to was passed and came into operation in October of that year. The Commissioners are 12 in number, and are selected by Government to represent the interests of Govern ment, the Municipality, and the Mercantile and Trading communities.

Prior to the constitution of this Trust, the Government itself, in the Public Works Department, commenced certain works of Port improvement, and the Commissioners, on taking charge, found four small Jetties for the use of sea-going vessels, and a wharf for inland vessels to load and discharge at.

During the ten years the Commissioners have had charge, the Jetty accommodation for sea-going vessels has been largely extended and improved, Hydraulic Crane Power introduced, and the whole of the bank along the river side, from the Bridge northward, has been reclaimed, and now forms a line of continuous wharfs along the bank of the river, with a public road 60 to 80 feet wide running along the whole length to the extreme northern limit of the Port; and, apart from the construction of public wharfs along the river bank, the Commissioners have thus opened out in the northern division of the Port a new means of communication which will prove most conducive to the convenience and health of this part of the town. Within the last twelve months the river embankment has been continued southward from the Jetties to Chandpal Ghât, and a double line of rails laid down by which country produce can be unloaded into the cargo boats at any point along the river bank. This embankment has reclaimed a considerable extent of unsightly mud flat that was exposed at low tides.

The Port Commissioner's railway connects the Jetties with the Eastern Bengal Railway at Chitpore, and with the Municipal Railway at Bagh Bazar. It is a little more than

2 miles in length, and crosses the Circular Canal by an Hydraulic lifting bridge.

The Commissioners are also Conservators of the Port, and in this capacity they control the movements of all vessels in the Port, provide pilots, moorings, &c., and take measures to secure the safety and convenience of vessels trading to the Port. The Commissioners were appointed to take charge of the Hooghly Bridge on its completion, and the maintenance and working of the Bridge is under their direct control. The Commissioners have now under contruction an embarkment and roadway on the western side of the river, which will be a work of great utility, and will vastly increase the value of property in Howrah. Financially, the operations of the Commissioners have proved eminently successful, and after providing several Reserve Funds it has been found possible to carry out a large portion of the Port Improvement Works from surplus revenue. The total amount of debt, for which the Commissioners are responsible to Government, inclusive of the cost of the Hooghly Bridge, amounts to about £800,000, and the re-payment of this debt within thirty years has been provided for.

THE HOOGHLY BRIDGE.

The Hooghly Bridge connects Calcutta and Howrah at a point a short distance north of the East Indian Railway Terminus, to which it forms a convenient approach. The communication with the Railway Terminus is toll-free; but a toll is charged on all local traffic between Calcutta and Howrah.

Owing to the great cost and time required for the construction of a fixed Bridge in a deep and rapid river with a treacherous bottom like the Hooghly, and dangerous from shipping breaking adrift, a Floating Bridge which could be cheaply and expeditiously constructed in the first instance, or repaired in case of accident, was preferred. The present structure is the first, and up to date, the only one of its kind affording headway for river navigation. It has cost 18 lakhs of Rupees, or at the rate of Rs. 20 per square foot of platform.

The Bridge is 1,530 feet long between the abutments, the roadway is 48 feet wide, with footpaths of seven feet each in width on both sides.

The platform is of timber, carried on longitudinal wrought-iron girders hinged together at the ends. These girders are supported at a sufficient height (24 feet above the water in the central portion) to afford headway for cargo boats and country craft by means of framed trusses of timber work, which rest upon the decks of wrought-iron pontoons. To secure stability, the pontoons are coupled together in pairs by means of the timber trusses. There are fourteen pairs of pontoons in all. Each pontoon is 160 feet long by 10 feet beam; the depth of the pontoons varies from 8 to 11 feet in proportion to the load they have to carry. Each pontoon is divided into eleven water-tight compartments by ten transverse bulk-heads, and is moored both up and down stream by 75 fathoms of 1¾ inch chain cable; the long scope of the cables allows the necessary play for the rise and fall of the tide. To preserve the line of the Bridge and prevent it from drifting up or down with the flood and ebb tides, the chain cables are hove taut and adjusted by powerful screw gearing.

The Bridge is connected with the abutments at either side of the river by adjusting girders of 160 feet span, so arranged that the platforms of the adjusting girders present an incline descending on to the Bridge at low water, and ascending at high water, while at half-tide the platforms are level.

An opening of 200 feet for the passage of shipping in the centre of the river is provided, when required, by removing two sections of the Bridge complete. These sections are connected with the fixed portions of the Bridge on either side by draw-bridges, which being run back by means of counterpoise weights leave the two central sections free to be warped out of position; these are first hauled a certain distance up stream, and then being disconnected are sheared one on either side clear of the opening. Vessels of over 200 tons passing the Bridge are required to use steam power. The Bridge is generally opened for the passage of shipping twice a week.

The construction of the Bridge was commenced in the beginning of 1873. The completion of the work was retarded for several months owing to an accident, whereby a large steamship was knocked out of her moorings and carried by the "bore" into collision with a portion of the Bridge which had just been finished, resulting in the total wreck of 250 feet of the Bridge, and sinking of four of the pontoons. Fortunately, the Bridge moorings held fast, otherwise further damage to the shipping, at that time lying above Bridge, must have resulted. However, notwithstanding the accident, the Bridge was completed and opened for traffic in October 1874, and being thrown open free of toll just at the period of the annual holiday, was a source of great delight to thousands of holiday folks by whom it was thronged day and night.

PUBLIC BUILDINGS.

FORT WILLIAM.

Fort William was commenced by Lord Clive immediately after the battle of Plassey in the year 1757, and was completed about the year 1773, at a cost of two millions sterling.

In form it is an irregular Octagon, with five sides towards the land, and three towards the river. It is surrounded by a dry ditch which, however, can be filled with water by a sluice from the river. The whole of the defences are faced and palisaded with great care, and are kept in admirable condition. The Fort mounts about 600 guns of various calibres. The works are very little raised above the surrounding country, and of course do not present an imposing appearance externally. The Fort is approached by six gateways,—St. George's Gate, the Treasury Gate, Chowringhee Gate, the Plassey Gate, Calcutta Gate, and the Water Gate; also, a Sally Port, between the water and St. George's Gates. Each of the gates has a house over it used as the residence of the Commander-in-Chief and of the Chief Staff Officers of the Garrison. Within are splendid ranges of Barracks for the accommodation of European and Native Troops, the Arsenal, Store-rooms, Magazines;

also extensive Parade Grounds. Entering from the Chowringhee Gate you pass through what was (before the Cyclone of 1864) a noble avenue of trees leading to the Governor's official residence (now used as a Soldier's Institute and Garrison School, still called "Government House,") adjoining which is St. Peter's Church erected in the year 1835, (commonly called the Fort Church). There is also a Roman Catholic Chapel, dedicated to St. Patrick, built in 1857.

The Garrison of the Fort consists of one European Regiment and one Regiment of Native Infantry, together with one Battery of Artillery, and the Lascars attached to the Arsenal and the Royal Artillery. The Fort is said to be capable of containing 10,000 men.

The Military prison is built on a massively-walled godown which bears a tablet with an inscription to this effect :—"This building contains 51,258 maunds of rice, and 20,023½ maunds of paddy, which were deposited by order of the Governor-General and Council under the inspection and charge of John Belli, agent for providing Victualling Stores to this Garrison, in the months of March, April, and May, 1782."

The Glacis and Esplanade is regarded as an appanage of the Fort, and is under the control of Government. It includes the space bounded by the Esplanade Row on the north, Chowringhee Road on the west, the River on the east, and Tolly's Nullah on the south.

GOVERNMENT HOUSE

Occupies a fine position on the north of the Esplanade, having a clear view of two miles over the maidan to the south. The grounds occupy about six acres, and are very prettily laid out to the south. There are entrances north and south, and fine gateways to the east and west.

Government House was built about the year 1804, (the first brick was laid 5th February, 1799) at the instance of the Marquis of Wellesley, then Governor-General. The architect was Captain Wyatt, of the Corps of Engineers, and the expense of erection about thirteen lakhs of Rupees, or about (in those days) £150,000. The idea of the design is taken from Keddlestone Hall, Derbyshire, which was built for Lord Scarsdale, by Robt. Adam. The resemblance between Government House and this building, however, does not extend beyond the plan, and, even as regards the plan, it is only in the main feature of a central building connected by galleries, with four out-lying blocks, which form wings, that any similarity exists. The internal arrangements are as unlike Keddlestone Hall as are the several elevations, or the roof. With all its faults, it may be considered a noble building, notwithstanding its want of height. The grand entrance is on the north side, by a handsome flight of steps leading to a grand portico which opens on to the first floor. It is seldom used except on State occasions, Receptions, and so forth; visitors generally using the entrance underneath the stairs. The interior arrangements are admirable, as far as convenience is concerned. The first floor of the central building consists of three splendid rooms; the vestibule entered from the portico, used also as a dining-room, the grand marble hall divided into a centre and two aisles by two rows of columns, beyond which is the throne room, opening on to a fine semi-circular verandah overlooking the grounds. The walls of these rooms and the pillars are of plain white chunam, highly polished, but the "coffered" ceilings are tastefully decorated in gold and colours after designs by Mr. H. H. Locke, the Principal of the School of Art. The *coup-d'œil*, when the rooms are lighted and filled with company, is splendid.

Above these rooms are the ball-rooms, the floors of which are of polished teak.

The four wings, which may be considered as distinct houses, are connected with the centre by means of commodious galleries. They are every way convenient and comfortable, and are occupied by the Governor-General and his suite.

The ground floor is chiefly occupied by offices; all the out-offices are placed on the other side of the road to the north.

The Council Chamber with its offices occupies the 2nd floor of the north-east wing.

There are a few interesting Historical Pictures in the building, among which may be noticed:

Her Majesty the Queen, in her regal robes, painted by Sir George Hayter. The picture is of colossal size, but as for the painting, the less said of it the better.

George the Third, and *Queen Charlotte*,—at the age of about 25, a very fine pair of full length portraits, supposed to be painted by Hudson (the Master of Sir Joshua Reynolds).

Louis Quinze (Louis Bien aime), and his *Queen*.—Very fine full length portraits, supposed to be by De la Roche. These pictures formerly hung in the "Old Court House," and were taken from the French; as were also *(from the same French ship)* the exceedingly handsome chandeliers with which Government House is furnished, and the twelve marble busts of the Cæsars which are arranged in the aisles of the Marble Hall,—probably the result of one of the successes of Admiral Watson.

Lord Clive.—Three quarter length, by Nathaniel Dance.

Warren Hastings ; fine full length portrait, seated ; artist unknown.

Lord Teignmouth, full length, by Hayes.

The Marquis Cornwallis, full length, by Home, R. A. (Home resided in Calcutta for 33 years.)

The Marquis of Wellesley, full length, by Home, R. A.

The Earl of Minto, full length, by Home, R. A.

The Marquis of Hastings, full lenth, by Hayes.

The Earl of Auckland, bust, by a Native Artist, from a Miniature.

Lord Metcalfe, full length, by Hayes.

The Earl of Ellenborough, full length, by Hayes.

The Marquis of Dalhousie, a very fine full length portrait, seated, by Sir John Watson Gordon.

The Earl of Mayo, full length, by an English Artist, from a photograph.

The Earl of Beaconsfield, full length.

Mr. John Adam, full lenth, sitting, by Sir Thomas Lawrence, a fine portrait in his best style.

Major-General Sir Arthur Wellesley, 1803, by Home, R. A., a very valuable portrait of the "Iron Duke" when in India.

Sir Eyre Coote, three-quarter length, by Chinnery.

Lady William Bentinck, full length, a charming picture, by Beechy.

The Nawab Sadut Ali Khan, full length, by Chinnery.

The Shah of Persia, 1798, a full length portrait.

Jeswunt Sing, Maharajah of Bhurtpore, full length, by Augier.

Shere Ali, Ameer of Cabul, Equestrian portrait, by W. M. White.

A very fine marble statue of the *Marquis of Wellesley*, by Bacon, junior, stands in the vestibule.

Opposite the south entrance is a fine brass gun captured in the Sikh war, and on either side two brass howitzers curiously ornamented with tiger's heads and claws, taken at Seringapatam.

Opposite the north entrance, is a trophy of guns taken from the Chinese, erected by Lord Ellenborough in commemoration of the peace of 1842.

On one side a brass howitzer, curiously ornamented, taken at Cabul; and on the other, a large ancient brass cannon taken at Hyderabad.

THE TOWN HALL.

On the Esplanade, to the west of Government House, is the Town Hall, erected by the inhabitants of Calcutta, in 1804, at a cost of seven lacs of Rupees. It is a fine building in the Doric style of architecture, with a magnificent flight of steps leading to a grand portico on the south. The carriage entrance is to the north under a fine covered portico. The building, consists of two stories, and is used for public Meetings, Concerts, and Balls. The great saloon occupies the centre of the building, and is 162 feet in length by 65 feet in width. The lower floor is but little used at present. The south front consists of two corner rooms 43 feet by 21 feet, and a central one 82 feet by 30 feet. These are used as card or supper rooms. The height of the lower floor is 23 feet, and it is paved with marble. The upper apartments are boarded with teak throughout, and are 27 feet in height, They are reached from the northern vestibule by two spacious flights of stairs.

In the southern vestibule is placed a fine marble statue of *Warren Hastings*, by R. Westmacott, R. A.

At the west end of the lower saloon is a superb marble statue, by J. Bacon, Junr., to the memory of *The Marquis of Cornwallis*, bearing the following inscription :—

"In honour of the Most Noble the Marquis of Cornwallis, K. G., Governor-General of India, September 1786 to October 1793, who by an administration uniformly conducted on the principles of wisdom, equity, and sound policy, improved the internal resources of the country, promoted the happiness of its inhabitants, conciliated the friendship of the foreign powers, confirmed the attachment of the allies of the Company, and established the reputation of the British name in Hindustan for good faith and moderation. By fixing in perpetuity the public demand for the landed revenue, he gave to the proprietor of the soil for the first time a permanent interest in it ; and by the formation of a code of regulations for every department of the Government, he bestowed on the natives of India the benefit of a constitution and a security before unknown in the enjoyment of their rights of property. Forced into a war by the unprovoked aggression of Tippoo Sultan, his eminent military talents in the conduct of it were no less conspicuous than his moderation in victory. As a lasting memorial of these important services, and as a testimony of their respect and esteem for a Governor-General under whose administration public spirit was encouraged and merit liberally rewarded, this statue was erected by the British inhabitants of Bengal, A. D. 1803."

In the north vestibule are busts of *C. B. Greenlaw, Esq.*, Secretary to the Marine Board, erected by the community of British India, to commemorate the energy with which, for twenty years, he advocated the cause of Steam Communication, and finally succeeded in its establishment; and of *John Palmer, Esq.*, Merchant, erected by a numerous circle of friends, European and Native.

In the south saloon, are fine full length portraits of *Queen Victoria* and the *late Prince Consort*, presented by Her Majesty to the Town of Calcutta, through Baboo Dwarkanath Tagore.

In the vestibule and staircase are a splendid equestrian portrait of *Lord Lake*, fine full length portraits of *Lord Gough, Sir Charles Metcalfe, Sir Henry Durand, Baboo Dwarkanath Tagore, Bishop Wilson, Mr. Cameron, Mr. Wilberforce Bird, Sir Henry Norman, Mr. J. B. Roberts, &c.*

LEGISLATIVE COUNCIL OFFICE.

Adjoining the Town Hall, to the north-west, is the Legislative Council Office, which contains the Council Chamber in which the Bengal Council assembles. The south front has a fine row of Corinthian columns, and the building is convenient and commodious.

THE HIGH COURT.

A little further west is the New High Court, completed in May, 1872, from designs by the late Mr. Walter Granville, Government Architect. It is erected on the site of the old Supreme Court, and accommodates both the Courts of Original Jurisdiction and the Appeal Courts (known as the "Sudder Dewani Adalat") formerly held in the large building at Alipore, west of the Race Course, now used as the Military Hospital. The idea of the building appears to have been taken from the Town Hall at *Ypres*, with such modifications as were necessary to adapt it to the purpose for which it was designed. It is in the Gothic style of architecture, and is faced with stone. The lower story of the south front has a grand colonnade, the capitals of the pillars are of Caen stone, beautifully sculptured, each one being of a different design. In the centre is a massive tower, underneath which is the principal entrance, through which we pass into a magnificent quadrangle surrounded by buildings, protected by a fine colonnade. The principal staircase is in the tower, and is of fine proportions; a fine statue of SIR EDWARD HYDE EAST, by *Chantrey*, is placed there. The carriage entrance for the public, is to the east, and there are private entrances for the Judges to the east and west. The ground floor is devoted to offices. On the first floor are the courts, seven in number; the Judges' and Barristers' rooms; the Judges' Library and the Bar Library, the Pleaders' rooms, and the Attorneys' Association Rooms, besides other necessary offices. On the upper floor are the offices of the Administrator-General, the Court Receiver, the Legal Remembrancer, and the Advocate-General's Chambers, &c., &c.

The Judges' Library is a room of magnificent proportions, and contains several fine portraits of the Judges of past days, most of which occupied the Grand Jury room in the old building.

In the Courts are also some fine portraits, a list of which is given below.

IN THE JUDGES' LIBRARY, full-length Portraits of

John Herbert Harington, Esq., C. S.

The Hon'ble C. Binny Trevor, C. S.

The Hon'ble John Russell Colvin, C. S., (afterwards Lieut.-Governor of the N.-W. Provinces.)

Sir Edward Ryan, Chief Justice, by *Sir Martin Archer Shee.*

Sir Lawrence Peel, Chief Justice, by *Grant.*

Sir Robert Chambers, Chief Justice, (half-length) by *Davis.*

IN THE PRINCIPAL COURT, Appellate side, full length Portraits of

Sir Elijah Impey, Chief Justice, by *Zoffany.*

Sir Henry Russell, Chief Justice, by *Chinnery.*

Sir John Anstruther, Bart., Chief Justice.

IN THE SECOND BRANCH COURT, Appellate side, (to the west of the principal staircase) a full length Portrait of

The Hon'ble Sumbhoonath Pundit, (the first Native Judge who sat on the Bench of the High Court, his predecessor, Baboo Ramapersaud Roy, having died without taking his seat.)

IN THE PRINCIPAL COURT on the original side, (East) full length Portraits of

Sir Elijah Impey, Chief Justice, by *Kettle.*

Sir William Burroughs, Bart., Chief Justice, by *Sir Thomas Lawrence.*

Sir Francis Workman Macnaughten, by *Chinnery.*

The Court at the persent time is constituted of a Chief

Justice and ten Puisne Judges. Of these the Chief Justice and four Judges are Barristers, five are members of the Covenanted Civil Service, and one is a native gentleman late a leading Pleader of the Court. They are all equal in regard to judicial authority and duty; but the Chief Justice is head of the Court, and has the control of the establishment in its various branches; the Puisne Judges rank after him according to the order of their respective appointments.

The general jurisdiction of the Court extends over Bengal Proper, Behar, Orissa, Chota Nagpore, and Assam, thns covering an area of about 245,000 square miles, *(i. e.,* an area more than four times that of England and Wales) with a population of (according to the 1871 Census returns) some 66 millions of people.

This jurisdiction is largely administrative as well as judicial, because in the absence of a Governmental Department of justice, much of the management of the Local Courts is entrusted to the High Court.

The Judicial work divides itself broadly into two classes, *original* and *appellate.* The *original* is that which comes before the court as a Court of first Instance, and may be said to be limited territorially to the Town of Calcutta. The *appellate* consists of all matters, very heterogeneous in kind, criminal and civil, which are brought before the court by way of appeal or for revision, from the District and other subordinate courts.

For the disposal of the judicial work, original and appellate, the Court sub-divides itself into specified Benches of one, two, or more judges in each, according to the character of the work which the Bench is intended to take; only that the decision of a Bench which is constituted of but one Judge (as is usually the case for original work) is not necessarily the final decision of the Court: an appeal from it lies to a larger Bench of two or more Judges.

For administrative work, the Court acts by committees.

The High Court was formed in 1862, by the union of the Supreme Court with the Sudder Dewani Adalat. Both these Courts have had an illustrious history, which can be barely touched upon here.

The first was created, by the celebrated Charter of 26th March, 1774, a Court of Chancery and a Court of Queen's Bench in one, consisting of a Chief Justice and three Puisne Judges drawn from the Bar of Westminster Hall, and having an exclusive criminal jurisdiction within the limits of Calcutta, as well as a certain general jurisdiction, founded on the personal status of the defendant, or on agreement of parties, thoughout the Presidency of Bengal. The leading purpose for which this tribunal was instituted was, that a ready-made substantive body of law, in the main coincident with the principles of English Common Law and Equity, should be introduced into the new settlement of Calcutta, and be carried into effect by a professionally trained court of co-ordinate rank with the Superior Courts of Westminster Hall, and that, through the authority and power of this court, independent of the local Government, all Englishmen thoughout the country, whether official or other, should be rendered responsible for their relations and behaviour to the native population according to those principles.

On the whole, in spite of certain early extravagancies, the Court discharged its very difficult and exalted duty with great temper and success. The list of its Judges, from Sir

Elijah Impey to Sir Barnes Peacock, contains names which stand distinguished on the roll of the English Bar; and it is hardly too much to say that the Supreme Court so taught the people of Bengal to understand the reign of law that the lesson will never again be unlearned.

The career of the Sudder Dewani Adalat commenced in 1772, when the East India Company undertook the administration of civil and criminal justice throughout Bengal, Behar, and Orissa, on a plan drawn up by Mr. Hastings and four Members of the Council; by which plan an ultimate Court of Sudder Dewani Adalat was instituted at the Presidency, under the superintendence of three or more Members of the Council, to hear appeals from the Provincial Courts in causes exceeding five hundred rupees.

In 1780, the avocations of the Governor-General and the Members of the Council having prevented their sitting in the Court of Sudder Dewani Adalat, the celebrated Sir Elijah Impey was induced, in addition to the Chief Justiceship of the Supreme Court, to allow himself to be made sole Judge of the Sudder Dewani Adalat. Sir Elijah at once framed rules for the regulation and guidance of all the subordinate local courts and for directing their practice; and it may be said that these still constitute the ground-work of the Mofussil system of administration of justice. Two years afterwards, the superintendence of this court was, on a resolution of the Home Legislature, re-assumed by the Govenor-General and Council. In 1801 it was enacted that the Court of Sudder Dewani Adalat should consist of three judges, namely, a Chief Judge to be selected from the members of the Supreme Council, and two Puisne Judges to be selected from the covenanted civil servants of the Company. And in 1805 it was found inconvenient that even the office of Chief Judge should be held by a member of the Supreme Council, and the Governor-General in Council was directed to select that officer from among the civil covenanted servants of the Company, not being members of the Supreme Council. This arrangement was afterwards again changed, and again once more re-established. And at the time of the union of the two courts in 1862, which has been mentioned, the Sudder Dewani Adalat consisted of four Judges in all.

At the outset in 1772 the work of the Mofussil Courts was necessarily somewhat crude. The administration of justice under the new system seems, however, to have become rapidly better and more satisfactory to the people than that under the native rule. Gradually, too, the education and example afforded by the Supreme Court had their effect. By degrees the method and practice developed under the superintendence and direction of the Sudder Dewani Adalut assimilated itself, though imperfectly, to the European model; and after nearly 90 years' experience it was judged best to replace the double machinery just described, by one comprehensive organization, which should be presided over by an English Barrister, and be largely composed of professional ingredients. How this has worked in the 17 years during which it has been in operation, and what are the results which it bids fair to bring about, are large questions, but have no place in these pages.

THE SMALL CAUSE COURT.

This Building is situated on the north side of Hare Street, on the site of the Old Post Office. It was designed by Mr. William White, architect, during the short time he was attached to the Public Works Department, in Calcutta. The architecture partakes of the early French style; it may be called French Palladian, with a slight leaning towards "Victorian" or 19th century work. The style is bold, and well adapted to the purpose of the building, and the interior arrangements are very complete and compact. It was commenced in July, 1872, and the main portion was finished and opened, without any public ceremony, in June, 1874. It was erected entirely by the Public Works Department. The building is 245 feet long, with an average width of 60 feet, and consists of three stories. There are fine north and south verandahs to each floor,—and the Courts are comparatively cool even in the hottest weather. The ground floor is 18 feet high; the 1st and 2nd floors, 25 feet high. The public entrance is by the east face, in Bankshall Street, and leads into a corridor, on the south of which are the various offices of the Court. A fine marble bust of the late Babu Hurrochunder Ghose, formerly one of the Judges of the Court, faces the entrance. A broad flight of stairs at each end gives access to the Courts, of which there are three on the first floor—one 28 feet by 60 feet and two of 28 feet by 48 feet; and two of the same dimensions on the second floor; besides a spacious Library at the east end. Each Court has a separate witness room, and Judges' retiring room attached, the latter opening into the south verandah, which is kept entirely for the use of the Judges.

The Judges' entrance is by a flight of steps at the west end of the south verandah, from which a private staircase leads to the Court rooms on the two upper floors. The Office establishment have a separate entrance at the east end of this verandah, into which all the Office rooms have access.

The Small Cause Court was constituted under Act IX of 1850 for the recovery of Debts and Demands to the amount of Rs. 500. By a subsequent Act the amount was extended to Rs. 1000. It is presided over by five Judges, the first of whom must always be a Barrister-at-Law. The working of the Court has been uniformly succesful, and results in a considerable annual revenue to Government.

THE CURRENCY OFFICE.

On the east side of the Square, is a lofty building in the Italian style of Architecture. The ground floor is the Office of Issue and Exchange of Government Paper Currency, and is worthy of a visit. The entrance has a very handsome gate, in three parts, of a very florid design, in wrought iron. The central hall is of very grand proportions, and is lighted by sky lights surmounting three large domes. Here are the exchange counters for notes, gold, silver, and small change. To the left as you walk up the hall is a noble array of huge iron safes full of new note forms representing the value of many millions. The bulk of the silver is kept in strong vaults in Fort William, but a working reserve is kept in the Currency Office, in a vault of massive masonry lined throughout, roof, walls, and floor, with iron; an iron door six inches in thickness closes this room, which is further protected by a second iron door, and last of all by a massive iron grating.

The rooms above are very massively and handsomely finished, and are floored throughout with Italian marble, even to the third story. Here is the residence of the Assistant

Commissioner in charge of the Currency Office. The building was originally erected for the Agra and Masterman's Bank, and on the collapse of that institution (soon after its completion) it was sold to Government, who were at that time on the look out for a suitable building for the Currency Department.

THE MINT

Is situated on the River Bank at Nimtollah, and is well worth a visit. It was erected in 1824-30 on alluvial ground gained from the river. The Architect was Major W. N. Forbes, Bengal Engineers. The foundations were laid at an average depth of 25 feet below the level of Clive Street, so that there is as much brick-work below as above the surface. The Architecture is Grecian Doric, the central portico, towards the Strand, being a copy on half dimensions of the temple of Minerva at Athens.

The Mint consists of two separate blocks of buildings, the one to the south called the Silver Mint, and the other to the north the Copper Mint, which was added in 1865. The two Mints taken together make the largest coinage buildings in the world. The buildings and grounds attached cover an area of 18½ acres or 56 beegahs. The large two storied building on the left is occupied by the Mechanical Engineers attached to the Mint, and that on the right by the Military and Police Guards. Further on is the tank that supplies water to the Mint engines and on the opposite side of the road, the quarters occupied by the Warder in charge of the Mint gate, by whom visitors to the Mint are received in the first instance. Visitors are admitted only on Thursday.

On receiving his card of admission, a burkundaz is appointed to shew the visitor round the premises. He first visits the Merchants' Bullion Depôt, where bullion and coin tendered to the Mint for coinage are deposited. Here rectangular blocks of silver four to five inches thick are cut into pieces by the steam hammer. If Coin is tendered for coinage, he will be conducted to the Merchants' Melting Room adjoining, where the silver is undergoing fusion in huge plumbago crucibles, in furnaces heated with coke. When perfectly liquid, which occurs in about three hours, the pots are lifted out of the furnaces by powerful cranes and swung round and the contents of the pots are poured out into iron moulds. On opening these the visitor will see large ingots of silver or gold, as the case may be, standing upright like a file of soldiers. Each crucible contains 450 lbs. troy of silver, equal in value to 14,400 rupees. These ingots are next seized on by the men, who are gloved with coarse "gunnies," and dipped into troughs of cold water, whence they are taken out and the edges trimmed. In this room the Thermometer often rises to 140° Fahrenheit.

The Silver Mint building contains a similar room, which is approached through a narrow passage. In the centre of the quadrangle are the bullion vaults, in which all the silver and gold bullion of the various departments of the Mint is lodged.

We next enter the Bullion Room, where piles of silver are weighed out and put into separate boxes. This is called alligating the silver, that is, sharing silver of different qualities so as to produce silver of the standard quality required by law for the Indian coinage, *viz*.:—11 parts of pure silver, and one part of copper alloy. Here, while one official is weighing out silver to be melted and converted into coin, the other is weighing over the finished coin—the balances used being large ones, and so finely adjusted as to turn to the one-tenth of a grain with a load of 4,000 tolas, or 1,500 ounces troy.

In this room is a fine marble bust of Major-General Forbes, erected by the Honorable the Court of Directors of the East India Company.

The visitor next passes into the Melting Room. This is a duplicate of the Merchants' Melting Room, but on a larger scale; the furnaces here are also heated with coke. In the next room, the silver ingots are laminated, *i.e.*, drawn out into thin and narrow straps, being reduced from one to one-sixteenth of an inch. Here thick cakes of copper are likewise reduced to thin straps. These straps of metal are next conveyed to the fine rolling-room, when they are reduced to the proper thickness, and thence to the cutting room, where a fly wheel drives a number of screw presses into which the straps are thrust. The screw brings down a punch upon the strap and cuts a blank right through the metal, thrusting the blank into a recess below the cutter, which opens from below. Here the blanks are collected, weighed and bagged, and the bags passed on to the next (the Milling) Department, except the silver ones, which are sent to the adjusting room into which the visitor will afterwards be taken. In the Milling Department a machine with a couple of revolving discs raises the edges of the blanks and forms the rim. Particular attention is called to this neat little machine, which revolves so rapidly that the silver blanks fall from it in one continuous stream, and look as if a silver current was being poured out. After this the blanks are sent on to the Annealing Department, where they are heated in furnaces to a red heat with the view of restoring to them their original softness, and then they are dipped in an acid solution which renders their surfaces clean and blanched.

The visitor next enters the Coining Department, in which there are 12 screw presses, and at right-angles to them, in an adjoining room, 14 lever presses. In the former, the presses fall down on the blanks, giving them a blow which gets up the impression of the coin, while in the latter, the dies are pressed into the metal to raise the impression. The mint coins gold mohurs, 10 Rupee and 5 Rupee pieces- Silver Rupees, halves, quarters, and eighth Rupees, and Copper double, single and half Pice, and Pies; also, for the Straits and for Ceylon, cents, half and quarter cents, and five cent pieces. The noise in this room is deafening, and the visitor will be glad to leave it and see the Automaton Balances, where the gold and silver blanks after being cut are conveyed for sorting. These balances, on being fed with the blanks, as they are technically termed, undertake the duty of weighing each piece and separating the heavy- and light blanks from those that are of standard weight. For instance, the rupee should weigh 180 grains, but practically blanks cannot be cut by machinery with such exactitude that all may be of the standard weight. The Automaton sorts out all that are three-fourths of a grain within standard from those that are heavier or lighter than these; the heavy ones are afterwards reduced to the standard weights, and the light ones rejected and returned to the melting pot.

The visitor next passes on to the Engravers' room, where he will see how the engraver cuts into hard steel blocks, and gets up the requisite design. He will also see an Engraving Machine, which, on being set in motion, cuts the design into a steel block of the same pattern, but smaller than the sample die attached to it.

On the opposite side he will be shewn the Workshop of the Mint. Here all dies and implements required for coinage are made, repairs to machinery, and miscellaneous work of a general workshop executed. He will see a powerful hand screw press with a large fly wheel, in which the die cut by the engraver is fitted and made to strike other steel blocks which take off the impression by repeated blows: these latter are the dies that are attached to the stamping presses to get up the coins. This press is also used to strike medals required for schools.

During a heavy pressure of work the visitor may have the opportunity of seeing the Copper-Mint at work. The machinery here is similar to that in the Silver-Mint, there being laminating, milling and stamping machines ; but as this Mint was originally intended for coining copper only, the rolls are much larger and are driven by a pair of 50 Horse-Power Engines, the driving wheel of which is about 21 feet in diameter, and when at work makes 80 revolutions a minute. There are twelve screw presses in this Mint, making altogether 38 coining presses in the two Mints, capable of turning out three quarters of a million of coins, silver and copper, in a working day of seven hours. The Mint has actually coined nearly a million of coin in one day, in the year 1866, when there was a sudden demand.

CUSTOM HOUSE.

The Custom House stands at the north-east corner of Dalhousie Square. It was erected in 1820. Extensive godowns are attached, but the new Jetties have effected an entire revolution in the system of landing goods, and the godowns, formerly a scene of busy activity, are now mostly silent and unoccupied. The extent of the Commerce of the Port may be learned from the following figures :—

Exports in 1879-80, Rs. 35,52,99,176.

Imports in 1879-80, „ 25,69,74,106.

The amount of Customs duty realised in the same year was as follows :—

On Miscellaneous Goods—		Exports	Rs.	13,25,649.
Ditto	ditto	Imports	„	72,15,791.
The duty on imported Salt realised			„	2,25,75,082.

Near the Custom House is

THE BONDED WAREHOUSE.

The Bengal Bonded Warehouse was Incorporated by an Act of the Legislature in March 1838. The building is substantially built, no wood being used in its construction.

THE PORT OFFICE.

The Office of the "Commissioners for the Improvement of the Port of Calcutta" is a handsome building in the Italian style of Architecture, situated at the corner of Fairlie Place and the Strand Road. The ground floor is occupied by Jetty and Shipping offices. On the second floor are the

Port and Pilotage offices, a fine Board Room occupies the third floor, and the Engineer's residence forms the upper flat. In the tower at the south-west corner is an illuminated dial clock, and the tower is surmounted by a time ball which falls daily at 1 o'clock.

THE GOVERNMENT OF BENGAL SECRETARIAT.

The north side of Dalhousie Square is occupied by a range of buildings until recently known by the name of "Writers' Buildings." This row of three-storied houses was formerly used for the accommodation of the "writers" or clerks in the East India Company's Civil Service, during the first year of their arrival in India, but they have not been so occupied for the last sixty years.

The central portion was the "College of Fort William," at which the examination of students in the East India Company's Service took place. The duties of the college are now undertaken by a Board of Examiners.

This fine range of buildings has recently been extended to the north, by the erection of extensive blocks of offices, and to the south by a new and imposing façade 660 feet in length. The whole range, when completed, will accommodate all the offices of the *Bengal Secretariat*, appointment, financial, judicial, political, revenue and statistical, educational, public works, irrigation, and railway branches, the Heads of Departments being located in the Main Building, and the offices in the blocks at the back. The additions and alterations are estimated to cost 10 lakhs.

In the open space between the South-Eastern corner of

Writers' Buildings and the Post Office, now marked by a handsome Gas Light, formerly stood a Monument on which were inscribed the names of those who perished in the Black Hole in 1757.

EAST INDIAN RAILWAY NEW OFFICE BUILDINGS.

To the North of the Custom House, and occupying the south side of Fairlie Place, is the newly-erected East Indian Railway office. This Building accommodates the Office Staff of the E. I. Railway and the Office of the Consulting Engineer to the Government of India for guaranteed Railways. The Building occupies a plot of ground 400 feet long by about 180 feet wide. The Building has cost in its erection about 3½ lacs of rupees and is probably the cheapest amongst public buildings of Calcutta.

In style the composition is fairly pure classic, but utilitarianism slightly decorated, and that decoration plaster, has been almost strictly carried out. Stone has more largely been used in the construction than is customary in Calcutta. All the cornices, which are of great projection, are of stone, and are intended to be rain and sun-shades to the walls. The floors of the principal offices are of Opus Groecorum, a tessellated pavement in marble.

A totally new mode of construction has been adopted in the building in the utilization of worn out rails for columns and floor trusses; the floors are of brick and concrete arches throughout. The doors and windows are all hung to stone cills and pivoted so that no wooden door frames, a costly item in the repairs of a Bengal building, have been used in the Building. The building is absolutely fire proof. The work was begun January 1880, and in February 1881 all the offices were located.

The Building has been carried out from the designs and under the supervision of Mr. R. Roskell Bayne, M.R.I., and Mr. Bradford Leslie, C.E., the Chief Engineer and Agent to the Company.

The Building has a large open inner court 220 feet long by 50 feet wide, enclosed on the lower story and utilized as a Printing Office. The four corner Pavilions are 72 feet high, four stories in height—the fourth story being servants' residences open to an inner enclosed court, but hidden externally by the deep cornices. This cornice which is of stone and iron has a projection of 4′ 10″, and is taken from the cornice of the Farnese Palace at Rome. The cornice of the Portico is entirely of stone. The Offices are mostly very large rooms, 80 feet and 60 feet long—one room to the north is 220 feet long and over 30 feet wide.

An Italian mode of decoration in Plaster called in Italy Sgraffito work has been used. The four subject Panels on the N.-E. and S.-E. Pavilions are Architecture, Sculpture, Music and Commerce. The names on the buildings are the principal stations on the East Indian Railway.

At the north-east corner of the building will be found a small paved space, paved to mark the land belonging to the Building, but thrown open as a rounded corner to facilitate public foot traffic. On this paved space is a line recording the salient angle and extreme point of the north-east Bastion of old Fort William. During the excavation of the foundations for the Building the whole of the north curtain wall, N.-E. Bastion, portion of the N.-W. Bastion and a portion of the E. and W. curtain walls of old Fort William have been exposed to view. A careful record of them has been kept and forms the subject of a paper in the Journal of the Asiatic Society of Bengal contributed by Mr. Bayne. The measurement of the north curtain wall *exactly* coincides with Orme's dimension, *viz.*, 300 feet. If his other measurements are as accurate they would serve to identify the exact extent of the old Fort. The S.-E. bastion has been covered by the Post Office buildings, the S.-W. should still be discoverable if looked for.

Several points of interest were unearthed, the red plastered faces of the Bastions—propably the source of the name of the Dalhousie Square Tank, "Lall Diggee," or the red tank, the old carpenter's shop mentioned by Orme and Holwell, an old culvert and drain that drained the inside of the Fort, and an old water-gate to the river. One of the walls of the Building 220 feet long is built on the north curtain wall of the old Fort. A wall 4′ 6″ thick below ground and where the foundation was 2′ 0″ below the level of the rest of the buildings. The old Fort ground level was about 3′ 0″ below the present footpath level.

THE NEW POST OFFICE.

This handsome structure is situated on the west side of Dalhousie Square, at the corner of Coilah Ghât Street,—being a portion of the site of the old Fort of Calcutta. The removal of the old foundations was a work of great difficulty owing to the extreme hardness of the masonry, which, in many cases, could only be removed by blasting. The building was erected from designs by Mr. Walter B. Granville, architect to the Government of India. It was commenced about 1864, but it was not until the year 1868 that it was opend to the public. It consists of two lofty stories, the east and south fronts being faced with handsome Corinthian columns, flanked by massive piers, in which are the staircases. The south-east angle of the building is semi-circular, also faced with Corinthian columns,—leading to a lofty circular hall, in which are the public letter boxes. This is surmounted by a lofty lantern, crowned by a dome, which forms a handsome and conspicuous object. The building is approached by handsome flights of steps.

THE NEW TELEGRAPH OFFICE.

This extensive structure, one of the finest public buildings in the city, is situated at the corner of Dalhousie Square, south, and Old Court House Street, east. The original design was made in 1868 by Mr. Barnfather, Executive Engineer, assisted by Mr. Clark. The ground was cleared in 1870, but the building was not commenced till 1873, after the plans had been revised by Mr. Vivian, who then commenced the foundation.

The style of architecture is one admirably suited to the requirements of the climate, somewhat resembling its neighbour—the Currency Office—but differing in its external decorations.

The building stands upon a plinth, 4 feet 6 inches high, and consists of a main block facing Dalhousie Square, with a Tower at the east, and three wings—the East Wing facing Old Court House Street, the other two forming a Centre and West Wing; of these the main block and the East Wing are of three stories; the other wings two stories in height. The total height of the building is 66 feet above the plinth, and of the tower 120 feet.

The Principal Front faces Dalhousie Square. The windows of the ground floor are 6 feet broad, the lower portion being fitted with handsome cast-iron panels. The windows of the first floor have broad ventilators fixed underneath them. The upper floor has two light windows, fitted with light cast-iron panels. The central entrance is of handsome design. The columns are well proportioned; the balconies and cornices bold and rich in decoration, and general effect exceedingly good.

The East Front is protected throughout its whole length by a broad verandah, with openings exactly corresponding with the windows of the north front. Both fronts are adorned with handsome ballustrades and finials, of patent stone, manufactured by Messrs. Fornaro Brothers, on the "Coignet" system.

The Tower is carried up as a part of the main building as far as the roof, strengthened, however, at its four corners, by buttresses, which are continued to the top, although not originally intended to reach beyond the balcony level. At the west end of the north front, and at the south end of the east front, are very handsome cast-iron gates made by Messrs. Burn and Company, of this city.

The building is built entirely of brick; the whole of the plinths, cornices, columns, and mouldings are plastered with Portland cement. The remainder of the brick-work is pointed and cleaned down.

The caps of the columns and the string mouldings are made of a kind of "Terra Cotta," modelled on the premises. Casts were then taken in plaster of Paris, moulded in prepared clay brought from Barrackpore, burnt to a reddish brown, and finally painted with Silicate paint and fixed in place.

The public Entrance is in the centre of the north front; on the left of the vestibule is the "Stamp Office," on the right are the "Waiting" and "Enquiry Rooms," in front is a broad flight of steps leading to the "Receiving Room," from whence the messages are taken by means of a shoot to the "Signal Room." On the ground floor are also the "Despatch Office," the "Printing Office," and the "Battery Room," where is a "Gallery" supported by cast-iron columns, in which the "Batteries" are arranged. The rest of the ground floor is taken up by the apartments occupied by the "Superintendent of the Bengal Division," the "Check Office," the "Clerks'," "Record," "Bath," and "Tiffin rooms."

The "Establishment" entrance is by a broad flight of steps in Old Court House Street.

The Main Staircase is opposite the entrance in Old Court House Street; there is also a private staircase in Dalhousie Square, and two circular staircases. The principal staircase leads to the broad verandah which runs along the East Wing in Old Court House Street, and extends the entire length of the South face of the main building. Every office has a separate doorway opening on to one or other of these verandahs. The rooms abutting on the east verandah are occupied by the Clerks of the Director-General.

The Director-General, his Personal Assistant, the Deputy Director-General and his Assistants, the Comptroller-General, and the Superintendent of Construction occupy the rooms on the south verandah.

The Signal Room occupies the central wing, and is 96 feet long, 36 feet broad, and 25 feet high; the wires run under the floor in five stone troughs which are hidden by cast-iron covers and are level with its surface. They are then conveyed to one or other of the tables used by the signallers.

The West Wing is entirely taken up by the offices of the Compiler of Accounts.

At the south end of the East Wing is the Committee and Model room.

Five rooms in the East Wing of the second floor, and a portion of the main block, with a splendid verandah, 11 feet broad, running the whole length of the east front, is given up to the Signallers living on the spot.

It consists of a Lavatory, 57 feet by 18 feet, a Dining-room, 32 feet by 37 feet, and two Dormitories, one 40 feet by 32 feet, the other 44 feet by 26 feet.

The three rooms adjoining the Tower are used as a Library. The other portion of the main block is occupied by Assistant Superintendent and Telegraph-Masters.

THE METCALFE HALL,

At the south-west corner of Hare Street, on the Strand, was erected to perpetuate the recollection of the many public and private virtues of Sir Charles Metcalfe, who was Governor-General in 1836, and more particularly to signalize the last great act of his Indo-political life,—the emancipation of the Indian press. It was erected, partly by public subscription, and partly by contributions from the funds of Agricultural and Horticultural Society and the Calcutta Public Library, by which Institutions the building is now occupied. The foundation stone was laid with Masonic honors on the 19th December, 1840, and the building was completed in 1844.

The design is taken from the portico of the Temple of the Winds at Athens. The architect was Mr. C. K. Robinson, and the builders, Messrs. Burn and Co. The principal entrance is on the east, under a covered colonnade. Internally there are two stories—the lower one occupied by the Agricultural and Horticultural Society; the upper one, which is approached by a handsome flight of steps, by the Calcutta Public Library. Opposite the entrance is a fine bust of Sir Charles Metcalfe.

THE DALHOUSIE INSTITUTE

Is situated within Dalhousie Square, on the south side. Externally it has no pretensions to architectural beauty, but it contains a handsome hall, 90 feet by 45 feet, the walls of which are lined with marble, with a semi-circular roof, richly decorated. There is also a reading room attached. It was erected "as a monumental edifice, to contain within its walls statues and busts of great men." The Dalhousie Testimonial Fund, the Havelock, Neil and Nicholson Fund, and the Venables' Fund (raised to commemorate the heroic deeds of these distinguished men in the Mutiny of 1857) supplemented by public subscriptions to the extent of 30,000 rupees, were appropriated to its erection. The foundation was laid on the 4th March, 1865, with Masonic honors, in the presence of the Lieutenant-Governor of Bengal and a large assemblage.

The Hall is available for Lectures, Concerts, and other entertainments.

The entrance portico was erected in or about 1824 (the Institute building having been tacked on to it) and contains a fine statue of the *Marquis of Hastings*, by Chantrey, bearing the following inscription :—

"In honor of the Most Noble the Marquis of Hastings, K. G., Governor-General of British India, from the year of our Lord 1813 to 1823. Erected by the British Inhabitants of Calcutta."

In the Hall are the following statues and busts :—

The Marquis of Dalhousie, Governor-General of India from 1848 to 1856, erected in his honor by general subscription. A fine full length statue, by Steel, R. S. A.

The Right Honorable *James Wilson*, member of the Supreme Council, 1860. Full length statue by Steel, R. S. A.

Brigadier-General *J. G. S. Neil*, C. B. Bust by Noble.

Major-General *Sir Henry Havelock*, Bart., K. C. B. Bust by Noble.

Major-General *Sir James Outram*, K. C. B. Bust by Foley.

Edward E. Venables, Indigo Planter, Azimgurh. Bust by Steel, R. S. A.

Brigadier-General *John Nicholson*, C. B., who led the storm of Delhi, 1857. Bust by Foley.

CIVIL ENGINEERING COLLEGE, SEEBPORE.

To accommodate and extend the usefulness of the Civil Engineering branch of the Presidency College, the Government have recently acquired for two lakhs of rupees, from the Society for the Propagation of the Gospel, the well-known gothic building on the Seebpore bank of the river, called Bishop's College, which forms so striking an object in the view to those arriving in Calcutta by the river; a new site for a training institution for missionary deacons, &c., having been provided by taking up land at the junction of the Circular and Tollygunge Roads to the south of the Cathedral. A very extensive workshop having a *façade* in keeping with the old college has been erected to the northward.

Here the passed civil engineeriug students go through a course of mechanical engineering, performing with their own hands all the practical work of carpenters, fitters, &c. As the Civil Engineering College furnishes the Public Works Department, Municipalities, &c., with supervisors and overseers, the mechanical engineering course, supplemented by practical instruction in brick and tile-making at the Akra Government Factory, cannot but render them much more useful servants. The College affords excellent class-rooms and boarding accommodation for professors and passed students; and a native nobleman has offered to build quarters close by for students from the mofussil.

ECCLESIASTICAL BUILDINGS.

Calcutta is well supplied with church accommodation. There are no less than seventeen Protestant Churches and Chapels; eight Roman Catholic; and eight belonging to other Sects.

ST. PAUL'S CATHEDRAL

Occupies a fine site at the extreme south of the Maidan. So long ago as the year 1819, the idea of a Cathedral Church was entertained, and a design and plans on a grand scale were prepared, but the project fell through. Twenty years after it was revived by Bishop Wilson, who prosecuted it with characteristic energy. He applied to Government for a site, and the moment the present one was granted he took possession. A Committee was appointed, and on the 8th October, 1839, the foundation stone was laid.

The design and plans were prepared by Major W. N. Forbes, of the Bengal Engineers, and carried out under his superintendence. The style of the building is "Indo-gothic," that is to say, gothic adapted to the exigencies of the Indian climate. The extreme length of the building is 247 feet and its width 81, and at the Transepts 114. The height of the Tower and Spire from the ground is 201 feet, and of the Walls to the top of the battlements, 59 feet There is a grand enclosed verandah or porch to the west, 61 feet by 21 feet, over which is the Library. The Vestibule is 36 feet by 22 feet 8 inches. The lantern beneath the Tower is 27 feet square, and opens by lofty arches to the Transepts.

The dimensions of the main body of the Cathedral are 127 feet by 61 feet, and it is spanned by an iron-trussed roof, adorned with gothic tracery. The interior fittings are handsomely carved. The east window was the gift of the Dean and Chapter of Windsor. The subject is "the Crucifixion," after a design by West. It was originally intended as a present from King George the Third to St. George's Chapel, Windsor, but from some cause unknown was never erected in the place designed. It cost £4,000. The Communion plate was the gift of Her Majesty the Queen. The Reredos is a recent erection, and is not yet completed. A new organ built by Joseph Willis and Sons, of London, was opened on St. Paul's Day, January 23rd, 1881. It contains 41 stops, and is a remarkably fine Instrument. Full choral service is performed on Sunday by a carefully-trained choir, under the orgainst, Mr. T. Henry Webb. There is also a choral service on Wednesday evenings, and Matins and Vespers daily. The Clock was made by Vulliaumy, the chimes are very melodious. The great bell bears the inscription—"Its sound is gone out into all lands." The western light is occupied by a memorial window to the late Lord Mayo.

The Cathedral was consecrated on the 8th of October, 1847. The expenditure on the building was about 5 lakhs of Rupees (£50,000.) About £75,000 was raised, of which the Bishop gave £20,000—one lakh for the building and one for the endowment. The East India Company appointed two additional chaplains, gave the site, and contributed

£15,000 towards the building. The subcription raised in India amounted to £12,000; in England to £13,000, besides a grant from the Society for the Propagation of the Gospel of £5,000; one from the Society for the Promotion of Christian Knowledge of £5,000; and a gift from Mr. Thomas Nutt, of London, of £4,000.

There are some fine monuments in the Vestibule and Transept, the principal of which are here briefly indicated.

In the WESTERN VESTIBULE.

Major-General W. N. Forbes, the Architect of the Cathedral and the Mint, a marble tablet with two supporters, surmounted by a fine bust.

A fine marble Tablet to the memory of certain Officers who fell in the Indian Revolt of 1857. The names are engraved on a panel of black marble in the centre, surrounded by 16 bronze medallion portraits.

The Hon'ble John Paxton Norman, who was assassinated on the steps of the Town Hall, 20th September, 1871, a beautiful Gothic Mural Monument.

Under the TOWER ARCH.

A fine Gothic monument to the memory of *the Earl of Elgin*, Governor-General in 1861. At the top is a beautiful marble medallion portrait, and beneath, four fine bronze panels significant of the principal events in his career. The monument was erected by Government in recognition of the many eminent services rendered to his country in Jamaica, Canada, China and India.

Sir H. M. Lawrence, a very graceful marble tablet supported by Serpentine pillars, with white marble medallion portrait.

William Ritchie, formerly Advocate-General in Bengal, died 22nd March, 1862, a marble tablet surmounted by a finely executed bust.

In the South Transept.

Lady Canning's monument, removed from Barrackpore Park, where it was originally erected. It is an immense marble platform, ornamented with Mosaic work, and surmounted by a Cenotaph, with beautifully carved headstone. It is a fine work of art, but sadly out of place in its present position.

Sir William Hay Macnaghten, B. C. S., assassinated in Cabul in 1841. A fine mural tablet, supported by two full length figures of natives, and surmounted by a seated statue of Sir William Macnaghten in fine relief.

Sir H. M. Elliot, died 20th December, 1853, a white marble tablet.

In the North Transept.

Sir Robert Barlow, B. C. S., Judge of the Sudder Court, died January 21st, 1859, a marble tablet.

Bishop Heber, a superb monument in white statuary marble, a full length kneeling figure in full canonicals, by Chantrey, 1835. The base bears only the word "*Heber.*"

Colonel Baird Smith, Master of the Mint, died December 13th, 1861, a fine Cenotaph, with inlaid cross, surmounted by a gothic canopy.

One of the panels of the *Reredos* contains a tablet in Mosaic work to the memory of *George Lynch Cotton*, second Metropolitan of India, who was accidentally downed at Kooshtea, while on a visitation tour, October 6th, 1866.

On the other side of the east window is a white marble tablet to the memory of the *Right Reverend Daniel*, fifth Bishop and first Metropolitan of India, died 2nd January, 1858.

Bishop Wilson's remains are buried beneath the chancel of the Cathedral which is so greatly indebted to his munificence.

Over the Western Portico is

THE CATHEDRAL LIBRARY,

Containing a choice collection of books in Divinity and General Literature, the bulk of which were bequeathed by Bishop Wilson, but modern publications are from time to time added. The Library is open to the public on certain (not very stringent) conditions,—no small boon to those whose means do not enable them to stock their Libraries with the standard Literature of the day, and one for which, if for nothing else, the generous donor deserves to be remembered.

ST. JOHN'S CHURCH,

(The Old Cathedral)

Is simply a revival of the old St. John's Church, which was destroyed by Suraj-ud-Dowlah in 1757.

As soon as Calcutta began to enjoy repose from the troubles of that eventful year, the erection of a new church became an object of general desire. One plan after another was designed, but not carried out; and in the meantime a temporary place of worship was erected within the battered walls of the Old Fort. It was not, however, until the year 1782, that the inhabitants of Calcutta seriously determined to erect an edifice for Public Worship suitable to the capital of our Indian Empire. On the 18th December, 1783, the new Church Committee first met, and was attended by Governor Hastings and his Council. As the sum of Rs. 36,000 had been already subscribed, the Committee determined to commence the building. The Maharajah Nobokissen presented, in addition to the old burying ground, six begahs of land adjoining, valued at 30,000 Rupees. Lieutenant James Agg, of the Engineer corps, offered his services as architect, and superintended the construction of the building. The first stone was laid on the 6th of April, 1784, on the morning of which Mr. Wheler, the acting president, gave a public breakfast at the Court House, whence he proceeded, attended by the great officers of State, and the principal inhabitants of Calcutta, to the ground on which the sacred edifice was to be erected.

The total cost was nearly two lakhs of rupees, most of which was raised by voluntary contributions.

The Church was consecrated (by a special Act of consecration sent out by the Archbishop of Canterbury) on the 24th of June, 1787.

The Tower is built of stone, (said to have been brought from the ruins of Gour) and hence arises the native name, the *Pattharee Girja* or *Stone Church.* An Altarpiece, representing the Last Supper, was painted by *Sir John Zoffany*, and presented to the Church. It is a fine painting, and is now placed over the west entrance. All the figures in this picture are said to be from life. Our Saviour is represented by a Greek Clergyman, of the name of Parthenio, well-known in those days; the disciple John, leaning on his shoulder, by a still better known resident, Mr. Blaquire, for many years a Police Magistrate. Old Tulloh, the Auctioneer, sat for Judas without knowing it. Every one is from nature, part of the figure from one person, part from another. Zoffany, we are told always charged his pictures at Rs. 1,000 per figure; this, therefore, may be estimated as a gift of about Rs 13,000 to the Church. When he was leaving Calcutta, shortly after the completion of this picture, a proposition was made to present him with a ring of Rs. 5,000 in value, but the low state of the vestry fund not admitting of this, a handsome and appropriate letter was substituted, as a "testimonial of the respect in which they (the Committee) held his great abilities as an artist."

The Church was enlarged and improved under the auspices of Lord Minto in 1811, and in 1865 the building was futher improved by throwing out a new chancel. The Church provides sittings for 700 persons, and possesses a good organ.

The remains of *Bishop Middleton*, the first Bishop of Calcutta, were interred at the east end of the nave, where the altar then stood, on the 12th July, 1822, and a black tablet, inscribed T. F. M., marks the spot. The statue of *Bishop Heber*, now in St. Paul's Cathedral, formerly stood in the east portico of St. John's Church.

There are a few mural tablets in the Church, to the memory (among others) of *Dr. Turner*, Bishop of Calcutta, died in 1831; *Archdeacon Loring*, the first Archdeacon of the Diocese, died 1822; *Dr. Corrie*, Archdeacon of Calcutta, and Bishop of Madras, died 1837; *Dr. Twining*, an eminent medical man, (1835); the *Hon'ble John Adam*

(1819); *Lieutenant-Colonel Kirkpatrick*, and other names well-known in Indian History.

In the Church-yard is the tomb of *Job Charnock*, said to be the oldest piece of masonry in Calcutta. He died on the 10th January, 1692.

The slab bears the following inscription :—

"D. O. M.

"Jobus Charnock, Armigr Anglus et nup in hoc Regno Bengalensi, Dignissum Anglorum Agens. Mortalitatis suæ exuvias, sub hoc marmore deposuit, ut in spe beatæ resur rectionis ad Christi Judicis adventum obdormirent, qui, postquam in solo non suo peregrinatus esset diu reversus est domum suæ eternitatis decimo die Januarii, 1692."

Within the mausoleum are slabs to the memory of *William Hamilton*, Surgeon, died 1717, a name of historical interest; of *Admiral Watson*, who commanded the fleet at the Bombardment of Chandernagore in 1757, and others.

Hamilton's Monument bears the following inscription :

" Under this stone lies interred the body of
WILLIAM HAMILTON, Surgeon,
Who departed this life, 4th December, 1717.

" His memory ought to be dear to this nation, for the credit he gained the English, in curing Ferrukseer, the present King of Indostan, of a malignant distemper, by which he made his own name famous at the court of that great monarch, and without doubt, will perpetuate his memory as well in Great Britain, as other nations of Europe."

There is a similar inscription in Persian character.

At the base of this monument are laid a number of tablets removed from the adjoining ground, which was the old cemetery.

Among these is a stone slab, found on the 5th July, 1869, eighteen inches below the level of the Church-yard, over a brick-built grave, bearing the following inscription, in raised letters :—"Joseph Townsend, Pilot of the Ganges, died 26th June, 1737, aged 85 years."

Another tomb contains an inscription to the memory of *Mrs. Frances Johnson*, "the oldest British Resident in Calcutta," who died on the 3rd February, 1812, in the 87th year of her age, "universally beloved, respected, and revered." She was married four times, and one of her daughters married the Right Honorable Charles Jenkinson, afterwards Earl of Liverpool.

The large Cenotaph at the north-west angle of the Church was erected about 80 years ago, at the joint expense of Mr. William Cooper, then a member of Council, and Mr. George Hatch, of the Board of Revenue, to commemorate the memory of Major Thomas Bolton, who fell at Rampura on the 26th of October, 1794, after cutting down many of the enemy. Major Bolton commanded the 18th Regiment N. I. With him fell 13 other officers, besides 12 wounded, some of whom died of their wounds.

Strange to say, it bears no inscription whatever, neither is there any reference to the memorial in the records of the Church.

To the west of the Church are four plain monuments covering the remains of three Judges of the Supreme Court, Sir Henry Blosset, (1823) ; Sir Christopher Fuller, (1824) ; Sir Benjamin Malkin, (1837) ; and of Bishop Turner, (1831). He was the first who took steps to form the Diocesan Clergy Society. He also arranged the plan for the High School, now called "St. Paul's School," which was removed to Darjeeling in 1863.

THE OLD MISSION CHURCH.

(Commonly called "*The Lal Girja*,") was founded by the Revd. Mr. Kiernander in the year 1767, and was erected at his expense. It was consecrated on the 23rd December, 1770, and named *Beth-Tephillah*, or "*The House of Prayer.*" Kiernander was a Swedish Missionary, who came out to Cuddalore in the year 1740. Driven from thence, and despoiled of all his property, on the capture of that place by Count Lally, in 1758, he took refuge in Tranquebar, and in the following year arrived in Calcutta, and declared his intention of founding a Mission here.

He was well received, and his proposition favored by Colonel Clive and the other gentlemen of the Council. Also by the Chaplains at the settlement, who raised large subscriptions to enable him to carry on his work.

The architect of the Mission Church was Mr. Bontout de Mevell, a Dane, and the building cost its founder 60,000 Sicca Rupees, of which sum 1,818 Rupees only was presented in benefactions.

Mr. Kiernander lost his wife in June 1773. She left her jewels for the benefit of Beth-Tephillah. With the amount produced Mr. Kiernander founded a Mission School on his own ground, in the rear of the Church, capable of holding 250 children. Subsequently a parsonage house was erected.

In 1786, Mr. Kiernander fell into pecuniary difficulties, and the Church, with all its appurtenances, was placed under the seal of the Sheriff. At this crisis the late Charles

Grant, Esq., East India Director, stepped forward, and restored the Church to religious uses. He paid the sum at which it was appraised—ten thousand rupees—and the Church, Schools and Burying Ground were transferred, on the last day of October, 1787, to three trustees. Mr. Kiernander became Chaplain to the Dutch Settlement at Chinsurah, and returned from thence to Calcutta, in 1795, where he died, in 1799, at the advanced age of 88.

The Rev. David Brown then became Minister of the Mission Church, which office he zealously and gratuitously discharged for twenty-one years. The Beth-Tephillah of the aged Kiernander was a very different building to the "Old Church" of the present day. It has now become one of the ornaments of the "City of Palaces." But in 1787, it was a clumsy, unplastered brick edifice, of small dimensions, and choked up with old houses; and from being of a reddish colour, had the appellation given to it by the natives of the Red Church *(Lal Girja)* by which it is still known among them, although its walls are, and have been for nearly a century, of a light stone color. Within it was exceedingly uncouth, with a brick pulpit built against the wall, and its aisle of rough uncovered tiling. A few rude benches and pews of unpainted plank formed the general seats, with a small number of chairs, without pews, for the gentry; and it was calculated to accommodate only about two hundred persons. It was indeed most comfortless, and it was pronounced by the then Society of Calcutta, utterly unsuitable for the reception of an European congregation. Yet it was strongly built, of good masonry, and lofty, and appeared worthy of being made attractive to a larger assembly.

Encouraged and aided by the fine taste and scientific abilities of his respected friend, Mr. William Chambers, Mr. Brown was not long in making a beginning to enlarge and improve the building. * * * It was also gradually fitted up in a manner suitable to the climate, abundantly lighted, supplied with an excellent organ, and with a handsome pulpit and reading desk. The cost of the last alterations and repairs (in or about 1805) was £4,000, towards which Government contributed £1,800, and also granted an annual amount to defray the current expenses of organist, servants, lights, &c. At the close of 1808 a permanent Chaplain was appointed to the Church by which time the congregation had increased fourfold.

When Mr. Brown was appointed to the Senior Chaplaincy he also took a great interest in the enlargement and beautifying of the Presidency Church, (St John's) and during the time that Church was closed for these purposes the Governor-General and his suite, with the whole congregation, gladly availed themselves of the one kept open solely by Mr. Brown's fostering attentions. "And here *Britain's Wellington* has suffered the graceful tear stealing from the heart, to adorn his manly cheek, on being reminded, from this pulpit, that it was '*God who covered his head in the day of battle.*'—Ps. cxl., 7. * (*Memorial Sketches of the Rev. David Brown.*)

In the Church are tablets to the memory of the Rev. Henry Martyn; the Rev. David Brown, (for 25 years

* Mr. Brown's Sermon, at the Mission Church, preached on the anniversary of the Battle of Assaye, before the Marquis Wellesley and his brother, then Sir Arthur Wellesley.

Minister of the Church); the Right Rev. Daniel Corrie (formerly Archdeacon of Calcutta); Mr. Charles Grant, &c., &c.

ST. PETER'S CHURCH.

(Fort William.)

The Fort Church was completed in 1835. It is a handsome edifice, in the gothic style of architecture, very neatly fitted up. There is a fine east window, a carved reredos, and an oriel window over the west entrance, filled with stained glass, also a handsome marble pulpit and reading-desk.

The Church is expressly designed for the accommodation of the European Troops, but there are also sittings for the public. There is a good organ and choir.

The monuments are mostly to the memory of military men.

ST. JAMES' CHURCH.

(Lower Circular Road.)

The old St. James' Church was situated in the centre of the native part of the town, between Dhurrumtollah and Baitakhannah.

In the year 1858, the roof fell in, and it became a complete ruin. It was resolved to rebuild the Church in a more convenient locality. A new site was secured opposite the Female European Orphan Asylum. On 7th June, 1862, the Lieutenant-Governor laid the foundation stone of the Church and Schools, and the consecration of the former took place on the 25th July, 1864, (St. James' Day.)

The new Church, a Gothic structure of an early English character, with Norman details, is one of the largest Churches in Calcutta, measuring externally from East to West 244 feet and from North to South 194 feet, inclusive of porches, and it is 65 feet high. It is capable of accommodating 700 persons.

In plan the Church is cruciform, with two lofty towers, 128 feet high, flanking the western end; and large carriage porches to the transepts and west end.

The transepts are of equal height with the nave, the Chancel with its semi-circular apse being of a lesser height.

The aisles, which present on the outside a series of gabled roofs, are designed chiefly to afford protection from the direct rays of the sun; they are divided into two heights by groined arches, the lower portion being used as ambulatories, having outside doors for access and the free admission of air to the Church; the upper portion being utilized as galleries.

Light is admitted by a series of long lancet headed windows placed in pairs 20 feet from the level of the floor, and filled with various colored glass of an appropriate geometrical pattern. Ample exit for the vitiated air has been provided in the rose windows of the transepts and western end, and in small circular windows over each pair of windows.

The roof is of teak, the trusses being coupled and elaborately carved in the geometric decorated style. It is massive and looks very handsome.

At that part of the Church where the nave and transepts intersect, technically termed "the crossing," there is a groined roof which has been elegantly decorated.

The Church was designed by Mr. C. G. Wray, who superintended its execution till the walls were about twenty feet high, after which the Government Architect, Mr. Walter Granville, superintended the works till completion, making many important modifications in the original design.

The cost of the Church was about two lakhs of rupees, exclusive of the cost of the land, the funds being wholly provided by Government.

There is a peal of 8 bells for the tower worked by Warner's chiming apparatus. The bells and the clock were paid for by public subscription.

ST. THOMAS' CHURCH,

(Commonly called the Free School Church) is a neat building, attached to the Free School. It was erected chiefly through the instrumentality of Bishop Turner, the School Funds subscribing upwards of half a lakh towards the work. It is the property of the Governors of the Free School.

The foundation stone was laid by the Right Honorable Lady William Bentinck, on the 13th April, 1830. In October 1831, the Church, which was built by Mr. Parker, was reported finished, and it was opened on Sunday, the 20th November, 1831. On the 2nd February 1833, it was consecrated by Bishop Wilson.

This Church contains 685 seats, distributed into 56 pews, besides accommodation in the galleries for about 500 children.

ST. STEPHEN'S CHURCH, KIDDERPORE,

Is a small but elegant building, adjoining and attached to the Military Orphan School. It is very prettily situated and almost reminds one of a country Church in dear old England. It was built in the year 1846.

ST. PAUL'S MISSION CHURCH, SCOTT'S LANE.

Founded in 1878, is under the charge of the Cathedral Chaplains.

CHRIST'S CHURCH.

(Cornwallis Square).

TRINITY CHURCH.

(Amherst Street).

These Churches are in connection with the Church Missionary Society. The services are held in Bengali.

ST. SAVIOUR'S CHURCH,

(Wellesley Square,)

Belonged originally to the Church Missionary Society, and was sold by them to the Gospel Propagation Society.

ST. ANDREW'S CHURCH,

Called also "THE SCOTCH KIRK" or "THE KIRK," and by Natives "LAT SAHIB KI GIRJA."

This is a handsome Grecian building in connection with the Church of Scotland. The native name no doubt owes its origin to the ceremonial when the foundation stone was laid, and to the connection of Lord Moira with the Church through his wife the Countess of Loudoin and Moira.

The Church stands on or near the site of the Old Court

House, directly facing Old Court House Street. Occupying this prominent position, it forms, with its tall massive spire, one of the familiar features of the town. On the north and south there are elegant porticos, with lofty doric pillars; and on the north there is also a spacious carriage entrance, added at considerable expense by the congregation, with the consent of Government, in 1838.

The Scotch congregation was formed in 1815 by the Rev. James Bryce, (aferwards Dr. Bryce) a fine full length portrait of whom, by Sir John Watson Gordon, may be seen in the vestry. Service was conducted at first in the Asiatic Society's Hall, and afterwards in the Old College (? now the Exchange). Government having given a grant of one lakh of Rupees, besides the site, valued at Rs. 30,000. The laying of the foundation stone was fixed for St. Andrew's Day, (30th November) 1815. The Countess of Loudoun and Moira attended in state, and there was an imposing Masonic, Military, and Civic display.

After the foundation stone had been laid, and other forms gone though, Dr. Bryce addressed the Countess of Loudoun and spoke of the hereditary attachment of the family which she represented to the principles of the Church of Scotland, and the support they had given to her ecclesiastical polity in days of difficulty and danger. "To this address the Countess made a short and appropriate reply, expressive of the pleasure she felt in being present at so interesting a ceremony, and assuring the Kirk Session that they might depend on Her Ladyship's attachment to the Church of her native country." The builders were Messrs. Burn, Currie and Co. It was opened for public worship on 8th March, 1818.

The Kirk Session having resolutely set themselves to complete the Church in a proper style, in the faith that the money required would be got somehow, laid the floor with marble, completed the spire, erected a railing, improved the approaches, &c., &c., so that the entire cost was nearly a lakh in addition to the Government contribution. Subscriptions were readily forthcoming to the extent of Rs. 36,000, but with reference to the balance the Session found themselves in such serious difficulties that they were driven to apply to Government for the whole or part of the proceeds of a Lottery (!) basing their application on the ground that the Church might be considered one of the improvements to which the Lotteries were devoted. Government, however, having indicated in reply, that improvements calculated to secure the cleanliness and health of the town, and to add to the comfort and convenience of the inhabitants, were the objects principally considered in the appropriation of the Lottery, and that at any rate works of this kind had been sanctioned which would place Government considerably in advance to the fund, the Kirk Session were driven to issue Debentures, bearing high rates of interest, secured on the revenues of the Church. The effect of this was that the debt continued gradually to increase, and the final liquidation, under certain stringent conditions, was arranged for by Government, first of all by an advance, in 1823, and finally by an absolute payment, in 1834, of Rs. 80,000.

An interesting tradition hangs about the spire. Bishop Middleton, the first Bishop of Calcutta, believed that the Church of England had a monopoly of spires, not only in England but everywhere in the British dominions, Scotland perhaps excepted. Dr. Bryce who had been his fellow passenger from England, and whom, according to Mr. Kaye, he found to be even worse than his other main enemy the "prickly heat," was naturally of a different opinion, and on hearing that the Bishop had used his influence to prevent him from getting the sanction of Government to erect a spire, he declared that he would not only have a "steeple" higher than that of the Cathedral Church of St. John, but that he would place on the top of it a cock to crow over the Bishop, which came to pass accordingly. Government, it is alleged, as a salve to the Bishop's wound, directed that though the rest of the building might be repaired, this audacious bird should not have the benefit of the Public Works Department. In spite of this, or as cynical people might perhaps say *because of this*, the cock still continues to stand, and seems as capable as ever it was of crowing over any adversary.

"An Enharmonic Organ," much admired at the time, was placed in this Church, and this is probably the earliest instance of instrumental music having been successfully introduced into the service of the Church of Scotland. The original organ was replaced in 1858 by a much finer one, built by Messrs. Gray and Davison of London, at a cost of upwards of Rs. 10,000.

The Clock was placed in the Tower in 1835, Government having contributed Rs. 2,200, and the Public Rs. 2,700.

Monuments, &c.—Besides the painting of Dr. Bryce already referred to, there is in the Vestry a companion portrait of the Rev. Dr. Charles, who was the second to occupy the position of Senior Chaplain of the Church. There are also various marble monuments, amongst which may be mentioned those erected to the memory of the Rev. Dr. Brown (Dr. Bryce's colleague) who died at Malacca in 1830; the Rev. D. Meiklejohn (Dr. Charles' successor in the Senior Chaplaincy) who died at Calcutta in 1850; the Rev. Dr. Ogilvie, of the General Assembly's Institution, who died at Penang in 1871, and Mr. James Allan, of Dykes & Co., a very zealous Elder of the Church, and founder of the Vernacular School in Rawdon Street, now under the management of the Kirk Session.

Management.—The affairs of the Church are managed by the Kirk Session, consisting of a body of Elders, presided over by the Chaplain, or the Chaplains in turn, when there are two. This body, along with the corresponding bodies in Madras and Bombay, has the right of sending representatives to the General Assembly of the Church of Scotland which meets annually in Edinburgh, a privilege which the Imperial Parliament and the Church acting in concert have not conferred on any other branch of the Church of Scotland, except that in Holland.

FREE CHURCH.

(Wellesley Square.)

On news reaching Calcutta of the disruption that had taken place in the Church of Scotland, those who sympathised with this movement formed themselves into a congregation, and met for the first time as a separate body, for divine service on the 13th August, 1843, in the Freemasons' Hall, Bentinck Street. Dr. Duff, supported by all the other missionaries hitherto in connection with the Church of Scotland, officiated on the occasion. The Rev. John Macdonald, one of the missionaries, consented to act as their minister, until one should be got from home. At the same time it was resolved to erect a permanent place of worship, a Committee was appointed, and a subscription was opened for this purpose. While the Committee was in search of a temporary place, the Directors of the Parental Academic Institution, now the Doveton College, kindly offered the use of their Hall for that purpose. The Congregation accordingly met for divine worship in it until the new Church was opened in August 1848.

In December 1843, the site, comprising 2 beegahs 2½ cottahs, was bought at a cost of Rs. 8,850. In May 1844, a plan prepared by Captain Goodwyn, of the engineers, was adopted. The cost, exclusive of fittings, was estimated at Rs. 30,000. In January 1846, the building was fast approaching completion, the internal finishing alone remaining to be done, when, on the night of the 15th, the roof fell in, the brick pillars on each side of the centre aisle, which supported it, having given way. The whole building, save the spire was found in so unsatisfactory a condition, that the walls had to be taken down, and the foundations to be piled and relaid. A new plan was agreed upon, and the aisle pillars dispensed with. The contract for rebuilding it at Rs. 30,000, exclusive of subsequent additions, was put into the hands of professional builders. Some of the members of the congregation on this occasion came forward with wonderful liberality. In addition to previous subscriptions, Mr. Hawkins, C. S., gave Rs. 10,000 and lent other Rs. 15,000, at 5 per cent.; Dr. Nicolson gave Rs. 5,000; and several others Rs. 2,500 each, and these were afterwards supplemented, until the whole cost, amounting to Rs. 1,15,558 was subscribed, with the exception of

Rs. 5,000, received from the Colonial Committee in Edinburgh.

When finished, it looked, as it does still, the neatest Ecclesiastical building in Calcutta.

The Congregation, though small, has been remarkably liberal. From 1843 to 1874, they subscribed for congregational, missionary, and miscellaneous purposes Rupees 9,63,692.

THE BAPTIST CHAPEL.

(Lall Bazar.)

This Chapel was opened for Worship on the 1st of January, 1809. It was erected from funds collected and subscribed principally by the three celebrated Missionaries of Serampore—Carey, Marshman, and Ward, who were the first Pastors of the Church formed in connexion with it. The Chapel is situated in the midst of a dense population, and vigorous and successful efforts have been made to attract to it sailors and other Europeans of the poorer class who are to be found in the neighbourhood. It is supported by voluntary contributions.

THE BAPTIST CHAPEL.

(Circular Road.)

The Baptist Chapel, Circular Road, was erected in 1819 by the efforts of the Missionaries of the Society who first settled in Calcutta, and who were formerly known as "the Junior Brethren." These were Mr. Eustace Carey, a nephew of the celebrated Dr. Carey; Dr. Yates, so well known as a Biblical Translator and distinguished Orientalist; Mr Lawson, the first Pastor of the Church; Mr. Penney, the well-known teacher of the Benevolent Institution; and Mr. W. H. Pearce, the founder of the Baptist Mission Press. The Chapel is supported by voluntary contribution.

Adjoining the Chapel is the Baptist Mission Press, under the management of the Rev. G. H. Rouse, M. A. This Press is favorably known in connexion with many valuable works which have issued from it. In connexion with it is a Depository of the publications of the Bible Translation Society, where the Holy Scriptures in Sanskrit, Bengali, Hindi, Urdu, and Persian may be obtained. The Press has a Type Foundry, chiefly for the production of Oriental type.

The Baptist Missionary Society has an Educational Institution in South Road, Entally, where Bengali youths are educated up to the standard of the Entrance Examination of the Calcutta University. It is under the management of the Rev. G. Kerry.

THE UNION CHAPEL.

(43 & 44, *Dhurrumtollah.*)

This place of worship was opened in June 1821. The form of worship is that adopted by the Independents, and its form of Church Government is Congregational. The Bengal Auxiliary of the London Missionary Society are trustees of the Chapel property. The Minister is chosen by the Church members, and is not necessarily a Missionary. Christians of all evangelical denominations are admissible to the Lord's Supper; it being, as its name imports, a *Union Church*, consisting of Christians of all denominations who agree in the essential points of the Christian faith.

The Chapel is built in a plain Grecian style. The

interior is commodious and neat. It was erected and is supported by voluntary contribution. The congregation though a small one raise about Rs. 7,000 a year for congregational purposes. At the rear of the Chapel is a large room for Sunday School and social and congregational meetings. The Minister's house adjoins the Chapel.

THE HASTINGS' CHAPEL

Is in connection with the London Missionary Society, and its pulpit is supplied by the Missionaries of that Society.

THE WESLEYAN CHURCH,

(Sudder Street,)

Was erected from designs by Mr. A. T. Osmond, and is the first Wesleyan Church established in India. It is an airy and commodious building, very neatly fitted up. It was opened for public worship in October, 1866.

There is a neat parsonage house adjoining the Church.

AMERICAN EPISCOPAL METHODIST CHURCH.

This spacions building was erected in 1876 by Messrs. Mackintosh, Burn & Co. It has seat accommodation for about 1,300 people. Though working largely amongst the poorest class of the Eurasian community, the church is now entirely self supporting, and contributes funds liberally for Mission work.

ROMAN CATHOLIC CHURCHES.

THE CATHEDRAL (MURGHIHATTA.)

(15, *Portuguese Church Lane.)*

When Job Charnock settled in Calcutta in the year 1689, a few Portuguese followed him, and the English Government allotted them a piece of land on which the friars of the Order of St. Augustin erected a temporary chapel. In 1700 a brick chapel was erected, and enlarged in the year 1720. In the year 1796, the Portuguese determined to throw down their old church, and build a more spacious one in the modern style. The first stone of the new church was laid on the 12th March, 1797, and on the 27th November, 1799, it was consecrated and dedicated to *The Virgin Mary of Rosary*. The building cost 90,000 rupees, 30,000 of which was raised from the revenues of the church, the remainder from public subscription, all deficiencies being made up by the Baretto family—two opulent brothers, then the heads of the Portuguese community in Calcutta.

The Bishop's Palace adjoins the Cathedral, which is chiefly used on grand occasions, for the solemn and imposing ceremonies of the Catholic church. On such days the spacious building is too small for the faithful.

THE ROMAN CATHOLIC CHURCH,

(3 & 4, *Dhurrumtollah,*)

Was founded in the year 1832, by Mrs. Pascoa Baretto DeSouza, and dedicated to the *Sacred Heart of Jesus*. It is a neat building with a good portico to the north, and a lofty spire. Its three altars and floor are of marble. It is well situated, being in the very centre of the Catholic population.

ST. THOMAS' ROMAN CATHOLIC CHURCH,

(*Middleton Row,*)

Was erected in the year 1841. On the 11th November, in that year, the first stone was laid by Dr. Carew. It was built by subscription, the principal donor being Mr. John Lackersteen.

It is a handsome structure in the Italian style, and has three marble altars; the central one is surmounted by a beautiful and large stained glass window, and the two side ones by oil paintings.

Adjoining is the Convent of our Lady of Loretto.

The other Roman Catholic Churches are

St. PATRICK'S, in the Fort, erected in 1857, for the accommodation of the Garrison.

ST. XAVIER'S Chapel, 68, Bow-Bazar.

The CHURCH OF NOSSA SENHORA DAS DOSES, 147, Bow-Bazar.

ST. JOHN'S CHAPEL, Upper Circular Road.

ST. JOSEPH'S CHAPEL, for the Madrassees, built by Mr. Freitas, and consecrated by the late Dr. Vanheale in March, 1865.

THE ARMENIAN CHURCH OF ST. NAZARETH

Was founded in 1724, by national contribution, under the auspices of the Aga Nazar. The steeple was added in 1734, and it was further improved in the year 1790. The surplus revenues of the Church are appropriated to the relief of the poor. The Church is called "St. Nazareth's," in honor of the founder.

THE GREEK CHURCH

Was erected in the year 1780, and dedicated to the Transfiguration of our blessed Redeemer on Mount Tabor. The first eminent Greek who settled in Calcutta was Hadjee Alexios Argyree. In the year 1770 Argyree sailed as Interpreter in the ship *Alexander* from Calcutta, bound for Mocha and Jedda. They met with a severe gale, and the vessel was dismasted. At the moment of extreme danger, when all expected that the vessel would founder, Argyree made a solemn vow to heaven that if they survived the peril he would found a Church in Calcutta for the Grecian congregation. The ship arrived at Mocha, and on his return to Calcutta, Argyree obtained permission from the Government to establish a Greek Church. A small house was purchased for divine service. But death put a period to the further pious intentions of Argyree, and it was not until three years afterwards that the foundation of the present Church was laid. The purchase of the ground and the erection of the building cost 30,000 rupees, towards which the estate of Argyree and his family contributed a considerable sum, the remainder being made up by voluntary contributions, Mr. Hastings heading the subscription list with 2,000 rupees.

THE PARSI AGIAREE,

(18, *Doomtollah Street,*)

Was built by the late Rustomjee Cowasjee. The religious services are performed by five Andaroos priests.

HEBREW SYNAGOGUES.

NEVESHALAON.

(*No.* 9, *Old China Bazaar Lane.*)

NEVESHAANAN.

(New Synagogue, No. 27, Pollock Street.)

Built in 1857, by David Joseph Ezra, Esq., and Ezekiel Judah, Esq., at a cost of Rs. 50,000.

THE BRAHMO SOMAJ.

The Brahmo Somaj, or Theistic Church of India, owes its origin to the Rajah Ram Mohun Roy, a man of remarkable mind and noble character, who was the first Hindu reformer since the establishment of the British rule in this country. His vigorous and persevering exertions were the main cause of the abolition of the barbarous rite of Suttee; he was one of the foremost pioneers of native eduction, and his valuable suggestions contributed much to the reforms which took place in the early political administration of India.

His great ambition was to bring together men of all existing persuasions into a system of universal worship of the one true God, the common Father of all mankind. By degrees friends gathered round him to sympathize and coöperate in this aim, and after one or two unsuccessful attempts, he at length, in January 1830, founded, what was then called the Brahma Sobha or Brahmiya Samaj, in the city of Calcutta. He bought a house in the Chitpore Road, Jorasanko, endowed it with a small fund for the maintenance of public worship according to specified directions, and placed the whole in the hands of the trustees. The trust deed, after prohibiting all idolatry, and all secretarian controversy in the future services, laid down that "no sermon, preaching, discourse, prayer or hymns be delivered, made, or used in such worship, but such as have a tendency to the promotion of the contemplation of the Author and Preserver of the universe, to the promotion of charity, morality, piety, benevolence, virtue, and the strengthening of the bonds of union between men of all religious persuasions and creeds." But there was no attempt to organize a system of monotheistic faith, and what is yet more remarkable, not only was the divine service at the weekly meetings of the Somaj composed mainly of recitations and expositions of Vedic texts, but the reading of the Vedas took place in a private room where only Brahmins were allowed to be present.

For about ten years after Ram Mohun Roy left India, the Brahmo Somaj remained in a stationary condition. The church gradually lost its vitality and seemed to be fading away, until it fell into the hands of Debendra Nath Tagore, who, in 1842, joined the Brahmo Somaj. He had in 1839 established the Tattvabodhiny Sobha "to sustain the labours of Rajah Ram Mohun Roy by introducing gradually among the natives of this country the monotheistic system of divine worship inculcated in the original Hindu Scriptures." In 1843, this Society transferred its monthly meetings to the Brahmo Somaj; and confined itself solely to the work of propagating the Vedantic faith.

But there was as yet no definite organisation among its members, or those of the Brahmo Somaj, which could distinguish the new school of Vedantists as a distinct religious body. With a view to supply this want, Debendra Nath Tagore prepared the "Brahmic Covenant," containing a number of vows enjoining the renunciation of idolatry, the worship of the One Only God described in the Vedanta, and the practice of virtue. Debendra Nath and twenty of his friends were solemnly initiated into the Vedantic faith according to this form in 1843.

Thus was formed the nucleus of the Brahmo community, and by 1847 the number of covenanted Brahmos had reached to 767. Another important step soon followed. In 1845 the four Vedas were copied out and studied ; the result was to dispel the haze of infallibility that had surrounded those venerable scriptures, which were found to contain glaring theological errors. After much conflict with the party headed by Akhai Kumar Datta, the Brahmo Somaj abjured the infallibility of the Vedas ; the Vedantic element was eliminated from the Brahmic Covenant, the fundamental principles of Theism being substituted for it.

By a curious coincidence, the same transitional period that worked the downfall of Vedantism, brought a new stream of influence to blend with those already received, and the Brahmo Somaj received fresh power by the accession of its third great leader.

Keshub Chunder Sen joined the Somaj in 1858 when in his twentieth year. During the previous ten years the Somaj had made considerable progress ; branch Somajes had been established in different parts of Bengal. But the external social life of its members differed but little from that of their polytheistic countrymen. But now, under the joint influence of Debendra Nath Tagore and Keshub Chunder Sen, some practical reforms were introduced ; a marriage was celebrated without idolatrous rites in 1861, and similar changes were effected in the rites observed at birth and death.

In 1862, Keshub Chunder Sen was ordained minister of the Calcutta Brahmo Somaj. For five years Debendra Nath and his young colleague worked in harmony, but about the end of 1864 the underlying difference in their views and temperaments made hearty co-operation no longer possible. The rupture arose on the questions of the Sacred Thread and intermarriage between different castes. In October, 1865, a large number of the younger Brahmos "went out," and a year later were organized by Keshub Chunder Sen into a new body entitled the "Brahmo Somaj of India;" with a view to make it the centre of all theBrahmo Somajes throughout the country. No president was appointed; like the Scottish Covenanters they declared that the Lord alone was their head; but Keshub Chunder Sen was chosen to be their Secretary, and he has ever since been their chief leader.

In January 1868, the 38th Anniversary of the founding of the Brahmo Somaj, the first stone was laid of a new *Mandir* or Church for the "Progressive Brahmos," as the party headed by Keshub Chunder Sen is called. In 1870, Keshub Chunder Sen visited England, and on his return, put in practice some of the hints he had gathered in that country, and started what he called the "Indian Reform Association," a body of which the nucleus was taken from his own church, but which was declared to be open to men of all classes, races and creeds who would join to promote the social and moral reformation of the natives of India.

The Association is divided into five sections, *viz.*, (1), Female improvement; (2), Education; (3), Cheap Literature; (4), Temperance; (5), Charity. In the 1st Section, a Female Normal and Adult School was opened in February 1871, and in the following September a small Girl's School was attached to it.

Brahmo marriages being regarded as illegal, Keshub Chunder Sen applied to Sir John Lawrence to take their case into consideration, and in 1872, the Native Marriage Act became law. It is a simple measure of civil marriage, of which the chief conditions are these; (1), the parties must be unmarried; (2), the Bridegroom must have completed the age of 18, and the Bride that of 14; (3), the parties must not be related within certain degrees; (4), if either party is under twenty-one, he or she, (except in the case of a widow) must have the written consent of parent or guardian.

In the year 1878 a third secession in the ranks of the Brahmos took place, owing to Keshub Chunder Sen having married his daughter, eleven years of age, to the Maharaja of Kuch Bihar, idolatrous rites being observed at the ceremony. This occurence caused a great excitement amongst the Hindu community of Bengal, but especially amongst the Brahmos, who made great efforts to dissuade Keshub Chunder Sen from so far stultifying what had been his life's work. The result was a secession of a considerable number of the members of the Somaj of India who formed themselves into a new church under the name of the Adharan Brahmo Somaj. The Adharan sect, though numbering few, if any, wealthy members amongst its members, have been working actively during the last three years, and have built for themselves a Prayer Hall in College Street, have started a newspaper, and published many useful books and pamphlets. Their wives and daughters enjoy greater liberty and a higher average of education than that of any other native community in Bengal.

Neither has Keshub Chunder Sen been inactive during these years. By means of lectures, processions and other "revival" methods, many accessions have been added to his ranks, and the name of the Somaj has been changed to

"The New Dispensation." An elaborate ritual, consisting largely of idolatrous rites, with which have been mixed various imitations of Christian and Mohammadan ceremonials, has been introduced into the form of worship.

All three sects of the Brahmos show a large amount of literary activity, the Adi being represented by the *National Paper* (English, weekly) and the *Tattva Bodhiney Pattrica* (Bengali, weekly.) The New Dispensation is represented by the *Indian Mirror* (daily) the *New Dispensation* and *Sunday Mirror* (weekly) in English, and the *Dharma Tattva* (Bengali, weekly). The organ of the Sadharan Somaj is the *Brahmo Public Opinion* (English, weekly).

HINDU TEMPLES.

It may seem strange to the visitor to be told that there is no Hindu place of Public Worship in Calcutta. The shrine of the goddess Kali (who may be regarded as the patron saint of the city) is at Kalighat, on the banks of the "Nullah" or canal which leaves the Hooghly at Hastings Bridge. Thither on certain days thousands of Hindus flock to make their poojah to the goddess. But all daily worship is performed in the house, or on the river bank, at bathing time. The houses of some rich Hindus have a "Thakoor-baree" or "house for the god" attached, in which poojah is performed by the family priest, but there is not, so far as we are aware, any Hindu temple worth naming in the city. There are the ruins of a fine old temple in Chitpore Road, built about 1730.

MOHAMMADAN MOSQUES.

There is a fine Musjid or Mosque, at the corner of Dhurrumtollah Street, erected and endowed in 1842, by the late

Prince Golam Mahomed, (son of Tippoo Sultan). It forms a conspicuous object from the north end of Chowringhee Road. At noon and at sunset hundreds of Mohammadans may be seen kneeling in the verandah. It bears the following Inscription:—"This Musjid was erected during the Government of Lord Auckland, G. C. B., by the Prince Golam Mahomed, son of the late Tippoo Sultan, in gratitude to God and in commemoration of the Honorable Court of Directors, granting him the arrears of his stipend in 1840."

There are many other smaller Mosques, but none worthy of special notice.

THE JAIN TEMPLES.

From the Upper Circular Road, a little to the north of Beadon Street, Halsee Bagan Road strikes off to the east. At its point of departure stand two massive square pillars. On the sides facing the road there is an inscription on marble in four different characters intimating that this is the "Road to the Temple garden of Rai Buddree Dass, Bahadoor, Mookeem to His Excellency the Viceroy." Going along this road some 200 yards we meet the second of two lanes leading to the left, called "Buddree Dass' Temple Street," which leads directly to the gate of the first and most beautiful of two Jain temples placed on either side of the way. Being open to the public, we enter and find ourselves in one of the prettiest gardens in or around Calcutta. It is adorned with water, walks, flowers, statuary and houses, and platforms for feasting, singing and acting. But the great centre of attraction is the temple, by far the prettiest in Calcutta. There is nothing Hindu or Mohammadan that can bear any comparison with it as regards size and beauty. We make no attempt to describe it or its sister temple; but add that to the Calcutta sight-seer it will well repay a visit. The Jains who worship in these temples are chiefly Marwaris, whose annual procession from Burra Bazar to the temples is the richest and grandest that passes through the streets of Calcutta. The Calcutta Jains by the 1881 census number 1,848. They differ very materially from the Buddhists with whom they are frequently joined and still more from the Brahmins who serve in their temples. Their sacred place in Bengal is the hill of Parisnath.

BURIAL GROUNDS.

Some of the most striking phases in the history of a city may be learnt from its Burial Grounds. We have already alluded to the old Burial Ground, surrounding St. John's Church, wherein still remain the memorials of the founder of Calcutta, and of others whose names are intimately connected with its early history.

The South Park Street Burial Ground was opened in 1767, and has been closed for some years. In it rest the remains, *inter alia*,—of Augustus Cleveland, Esq., one of the noblest of the East India Company's servants, who died in 1784, at the early age of 29 years; of Sir William Jones, the eminent Oriental Scholar; of Colonel Kyd, distinguished for botanical researches; of Alexander Colvin, an eminent Merchant.

The North Park Street Burial Ground has also long been closed.

The French or Tiretta's Burial Ground, *Park Street.*

The Military Burial Ground, *Bhowanipore.*

The Portuguese Burial Ground, *Baitakhannah.*—In-the centre of the ground is a tablet, bearing the following inscription :—

"This Asylum for departed Catholics is the gift of JOSEPH BARETTO, Esq., the 8th of February, in 1786, and is now inscribed by the present Vicar and Church Wardens, in behalf of themselves, and the Parishioners of that Communion, as a just testimony of the gratitude for the pious and meritorious donation. May the God of Righteousness reward him and his posterity for ever."—" *Calcutta, 1st June, 1808.*"

The SCOTCH BURIAL GROUND.—This ground, situated at Kurriah, on the 24-Pergunnah side of Circular Road, near the Old Park Street Burial Ground, is the property of the Kirk Session. It was purchased in 1820, and considerably enlarged in 1858. Some members of the Baptist and Congregational Denominations having slightly aided the Members of St. Andrew's Church in bearing the large expense necessarily incurred at the outset, the privilege of burying on equal terms with the Members of the Scotch Church was conceded to them, and the same privilege has since been extended to others, the existing rule prescribing—"That the deceased must have been at the time of death a *bonâ fide* member of the Church of Scotland, or of one or other of the different bodies of Protestant Dissenters in Calcutta, or a known attendant on public worship in one or other of the churches indicated."

The NEW BURIAL GROUND, Circular Road, was opened in 1840. At the entrance are handsome monuments to the memory of Major-General Sir William Casement, K. C. B., member of the Supreme Council, who died in April, 1844; and of Sir W. H. Macnaghten, Bart., B. C. S., who was assassinated at Cabul in December, 1841.

RELIGIOUS SOCIETIES.

CALCUTTA DIOCESAN ADDITIONAL CLERGY SOCIETY.

(*Secretaries*—THE VEN. ARCHDEACON, AND REV. H. C. SPRING.)

SOCIETY FOR THE PROPAGATION OF THE GOSPEL IN FOREIGN PARTS,

CALCUTTA DIOCESAN COMMITTEE.

Honorary Secretary—REV. W. H. BRAY, M. A., (*Office—42, Free School Street.*)

CHURCH MISSIONARY SOCIETY,

(*10, Mission Row*).

(*Secretary*—REV. H. P. PARKER.)

MISSION OF THE CHURCH OF SCOTLAND.

(*Secretary*—REV. G. G. GILLAN, M. A.)

BENGAL MISSION OF THE FREE CHURCH OF SCOTLAND.

(*Mission House, 20, Cornwallis Square.*)

BENGAL AUXILIARY LONDON MISSIONARY SOCIETY.

(*216, Russapuglah Road.*)

(*Secretary*—REV. W. JOHNSON.)

v

CALCUTTA AUXILIARY BAPTIST MISSIONARY SOCIETY.

(24, Lower Circular Road, Town side.)

(*Secretary*—REV. G. H. ROUSE.)

SOCIETY FOR PROMOTING CHRISTIAN KNOWLEDGE.

(Depôt, 3, Hare Street.)

CALCUTTA AUXILIARY BIBLE SOCIETY.

(Depository, 22, Chowringhee Road.)

CALCUTTA CHRISTIAN TRACT AND BOOK SOCIETY.

(Tract Depository, 22, Chowringhee Road.)

AMERICAN ZENANA MISSION,

FOR PROMOTING CHRISTIANITY AND EDUCATION.

(140, Dhurrumtollah Street.)

THE AMERICAN UNITARIAN ASSOCIATION,

(77, Dhurrumtollah Street.)

EDUCATIONAL INSTITUTIONS.

In the year 1815, the late Sir Edward Hyde East, Chief Justice of Bengal, Baboo Budhinath Mookerji, a Hindu gentleman, and Mr. David Hare conceived the idea of founding a College in Calcutta for the education of native students. Acting upon this suggestion, various meetings were held, and it was resolved that an institution for promoting education be established, to be called the VIDIALYA or HINDU COLLEGE OF CALCUTTA, and that the GOVERNOR-GENERAL and the Members of the Supreme Council should be requested to become patrons of the institution. Sir Edward Hyde East accepted the office of President, and a Committee of European and Native gentlemen was appointed. The primary object of the institution was the tuition of Hindus in the English and Oriental languages, and in the literature and science of Europe. On the 20th January, 1817, the school was opened with twenty pupils. For the next six or seven years, so little were its advantages appreciated by the native community, that it was kept alive only by the indefatigable exertions of the founders. But in 1824, the Government resolved to found a College for the special purpose of reviving Sanskrit literature, and it was deemed advisable to erect a large and handsome building, to accommodate the classes of both the Sanskrit and English Institutions. The building, since known as

THE HINDU COLLEGE,

Which was erected at an expense of Rs 1,20,000, and occupies the north side of College Square, was opened in 1827. Further additions were subsequently made to it, involving an expenditure of about Rs 50,000. It is a handsome building of the Ionic order. The grand entrance is to the north. There are numerous class-rooms; and Professors of Law, Philosophy, Mathematics, and English Literature were appointed, and for many years the college pursued a successful course.

In the year 1855, the educational schemes of the Indian Government took a more complete form, and the PRESIDENCY COLLEGE was established, in which the Hindu College was merged. Subsequently, in 1857, the UNIVERSITY OF CALCUTTA was inaugurated, with which the Presidency College (in Arts, Law, and Civil Engineering), the Medical College, the Sanskrit College, the Madrissa, and other kindred institutions were affiliated. In this connection, a group of fine buildings has been erected in College Street. We notice first,

THE UNIVERSITY SENATE HOUSE,

A noble hall, 120 feet by 60, in which the Convocations of the University for conferring degrees, &c , are held. Adjoining it, is

THE HARE SCHOOL,

A handsome and commodious building erected out of the surplus fees of the students. It is entirely a self-supporting institution. Adjoining this structure, is

THE PRESIDENCY COLLEGE,

The foundation stone of which was laid by Sir George Campbell, in 1872. It is a plain substantial building occupying three sides of a square. The Presidency College is open to all classes of the community, and the course of instruction is adapted to the requirements of the University, for degrees in Arts, Law, and Civil Engineering. There is an admission fee of Rs 10, and the monthly tuition fee is Rs 12, except in the case of students holding junior scholarships, who pay only Rs 10. Seven scholarships are attached to the general department of the College, varying from Rs 30 to 50 per month. In the law department the schooling fees vary from 5 to 10 rupees, five rupees being in the 1st year class, and ten rupees in the 2nd and 3rd year classes. This department also is self-supporting. The schooling fee in the Civil Engineering Department is 5 rupees a month. There are five Government scholarships, which are awarded by the examination for the L. C. E. degree held by the University. These scholarships are tenable in the Public Works Department, where the students are required to undergo a practical training in their profession for two years.

THE SANSKRIT COLLEGE,

Is supported by Government, and is under the control of the Director of Public Instruction. It was founded in 1824, for the encouragement of the study of the Sanskrit Language and Literature, and at first Sanskrit was studied exclusively. All the students now learn Sanskrit and English. A valuable Sanskrit library is attached to the College.

THE MEDICAL COLLEGE

Was founded in 1834 by Lord William Bentinck, with the view of improving the wretched state of medical knowledge among the natives generally, by distributing over the country skilful practitioners in lieu of the miserable quacks who had previously formed the physicians of the native community. In 1835, the present buildings were erected. They comprise two spacious theatres, the larger of which is capable of accommodating 500 persons, apartments for the study of practical anatomy, a Laboratory, Museum and Library, and Barrack for the hospital apprentice class ; also houses for the Principal and resident Medical Officers.

Medicine and Surgery in all their branches are taught in the English manner, by a staff of fourteen professors. The certificate of having passed the first arts examination of the Calcutta University qualifies students for admission. The course of medical education extends over five years ; all who pass go out with the degree of Bachelor of Medicine. Last Session the strength of students was upward of 500. Previous to the removal of the Bengali class to the Campbell Medical School at Sealdah, and of the Military Class to the Temple Medical School at Bankipore, the total strength of students in the Medical College was between fourteen and fifteen hundred, of whom nearly eleven hundred paid for their education.

THE CALCUTTA MADRASSA

Was founded in the year 1781, by Warren Hastings, who, at his own expense, erected a building for the College. The object of the founder was to encourage the cultivation of Arabic learning, and to teach Mahomadan law. The College was not successful; but in 1820 it was remodelled, and the present building erected on the north side of Wellesley Square, at a cost of about a lakh and a half of rupees.

In 1829, an English Department was organised. It was at first composed entirely of scholars on the Madrassa foundation, but was shortly thrown open to Mahomadans of all classes.

In 1854, an Anglo-Persian Department was formed; and the system of education in the Arabic Department was altered; *viz.*, the teaching of the Arabic sciences was discontinued, the subjects taught being chiefly the Arabic language and literature, and Mahomadan law.

Since 1863, a college class has been added, to enable students of the Anglo-Persian Department passing the entrance examination, and electing to join the Arabic Department, to continue their English studies with a view to appear at the higher University Examinations.

BISHOP'S COLLEGE,

Situated at Seebpore, opposite Garden Reach, presents a striking appearance from the river. It was founded under the auspices of the Society for the Propagation of the Gospel in foreign parts, on the urgent request of Bishop Middleton, by whom the foundation stone was laid on the 15th December, 1820. It is a gothic structure—forming three sides of a quadrangle. The side facing the river has a Central Tower, 65 feet in height, on the west of which are the Hall and Library, and on the east the Chapel, which is an elegant building with arched roof and tessellated pavement.

Two wings, each 150 feet in length, extend north and south toward the river; these contain the residences of the professors and students. The edifice cost above £15,000, of which £5,000 was contributed by the S. P. G. Society, and similar sums by the Christian Knowledge and Church Missionary Societies. Government presented the site. The College is under a Principal and Professors from the English Universities.

It was founded for the purpose of (1,) instructing native and other youths in the doctrine and discipline of Christ's Church, with a view to their becoming Preachers, Catechists or School Masters; (2,) extending the benefits of education generally; (3,) translating the Scriptures, Liturgy, and other religious works; and (4,) forming a residence for European Missionaries on their arrival in India.

In 1830, the statutes were modified so as to allow of the admission of lay or general students not intended for clerical or educational work.

The College possessed one fellowship and 21 scholarships. The holders of scholarships had rooms, boarding, and tui tion free of charge.

The College cannot be said to have fulfilled the intentions and hopes of its founders, and it has long been manifest, both to the public and to the Government, that so fine a building and so valuable a site was comparatively wasted on the few students who occupied it.

In 1879, therefore, the Establishment of Professors and Pupils was removed temporarily to the house No. 33 Circular Road, and the building and grounds known as Bishop's College were purchased by the Bengal Government for the sum of two lakhs of rupees in order to establish

THE SEEBPORE GOVERNMENT ENGINEERING COLLEGE AND WORKSHOP.

A very extensive Workshop having a *façade* in keeping with the College has recently been erected.

THE PARENTAL ACADEMIC INSTITUTION AND DOVETON COLLEGE,

(41, Free School Street, & 54, Park Street,)

AND

DOVETON INSTITUTION FOR YOUNG LADIES,

(35, Park Street.)

This Institution was established on the 1st March 1823, by John William Ricketts, "the Champion of the East Indian Community." The main objects in view were to effect an improvement in the defective system of education which then existed; and to provide for the Christian youths of Calcutta the benefit of a good education at a cheaper cost than it could then be obtained. The management was vested in a committee composed of parents and guardians and subscribers to the funds; and for years a large proportion of the Christian population owed their education to "The Parental." In 1854, a legacy of Rs. 2,30,000 * was bequeathed to the Institution by Captain John Doveton, and a College Department (named after the generous legator) was added and affiliated to the Calcutta University. An Infant and Juvenile Department, and a

* The bulk of this splendid legacy has unfortunately been spent, without any adequate advantage to the Institution.

school for Young Ladies were also formed in connection with it. The educational staff is strengthened, as necessity arises, by professors and masters from Great Britain. The Institution now numbers in all branches upwards of 500 pupils. In addition to a number of Government scholarships annually awarded to the students of the College, who pass high in the University Examinations, there is a Lawrence de Souza Scholarship for English Literature, of the value of Rs. 50 per mensem, tenable for one year, and also an Arson Scholarship of the value of Rs. 13 per mensem, also tenable for one year. The College Department likewise receives a grant-in-aid from the local Government.

LA MARTINIERE.

(*Circular Road.*)

Claude Martin was a native of Lyons, in France. He was originally a common soldier in the French Army, and fought under Count Lally. He afterwards entered the service of the East India Company, and rose to the rank of Major-General. He amassed a princely fortune, and died at Lucknow, on the 13th September, 1800. In his will he states his property to be £477,101. 12*s.* 10*d.*, and he makes the following bequests among others :—

Rupees 1,50,000, the interest of which is to be applied for the relief of the poor of Lucknow, Calcutta, and Chandernagore.

Rupees 2,00,000, to the Town of Calcutta, "to establish a school for the education of a certain number of children of any sex, to a certain age, and then to have them apprenticed to some profession, and married, when at age." And a further sum of Rs. 1,50,000, to add to the permanency of such Institution. Such institution to bear the name of "La Martiniere." It was left in the hands of the British Government to devise the best Institution for the public good.

The Funds were committed to the Supreme Court of Judicature in Calcutta, as the official guardian of all charitable bequests. And there they remained for more than thirty years; by which time, being placed at interest, the bequest had reached the amount of nearly 10 lakhs of rupees, or £100,000 sterling.

In the year 1832, a decree of the Supreme Court was promulgated, sanctioning the expenditure of £17,000, upon a suitable building, which was completed in 1835, at a cost of £23,000. It is of two stories, and is surmounted by a dome. In the centre of the building is the Chapel, and on either side are ample accommodations for teachers and children. There are two porticoes,—south and north, communicating with the chapel. Adjoining is a large and perfectly plain structure for the girls' department.

The Viceroy and Governor-General, the Chief Justice, the Bishop of Calcutta, the Commander-in-Chief, the Members of the Supreme Council, the Lieutenant-Governor of Bengal, and the Judges of the High Court, are *ex-officio* Governors, and there are four additional Governors chosen annually. The present Head Master is Mr. F. J. Biden, M. A. The Head Mistress, Miss Adams. There are 75 boys and 40 girls on the foundation, who are maintained, educated, and put out in life, in addition to whom a certain number are admitted on payment of a monthly fee. The Anniversary of General Martin's death is, in terms of his will, observed with peculiar honors. An appropriate sermon is preached to the children, after which an examination is held, and silver medals presented to the most deserving boy and girl in the room; all then adjourn to the dining room, where they partake of a sumptuous dinner and drink a toast to the memory of the founder.

There are similar Institutions at Lucknow and at Lyons.

FREE CHURCH INSTITUTION.

(74, *Nimtollah Street.*)

The Collegiate School and College, now located in this stately pile, was opened by Dr. Duff on the 13th July, 1830. The pupils present on the occasion were five boys ignorant of the veriest elements of education; they paid no fee; on the other hand they were regarded as conferring a favour on the great educational missionary by their presence. The school was opened in the house, now numbered 51, Upper Chitpore Road, then familiarly known as Feringhi Komul Bose's House. It is immediately to the south of the Adi Brahmo Somaj Mission House, the gift of Rajah Ram Mohun Roy, its founder, to whom the establishment of the school was largely due. It was in the same house that he inaugurated the Brahmo Somaj; and it was also to it that the Hindu College, now developed into the Presidency College and the Hare School, was removed from Gora Chund Bysack's house, where it had been opened in 1816 under the auspices of David Hare, and into which the subject of our present notice was removed in 1836.

In Gora Chand Bysack's house the Oriental Seminary has met, ever since the Missionary Institution left it.

In February 1837, the five boys had increased to upwards of 700, and in the meantime the instructive staff had been augmented by the arrival of the Rev. Messrs. Mackay, Ewart, Smith, and Macdonald. Dr. Duff had been compelled however to go home in search of health. While at home he devoted his time and talents to collecting money for the building of suitable accommodation for the school. On the 23rd of February of the above year, the foundation stone was laid, of what is still known as the General Assembly's Institution, in Cornwallis Square. The building was designed and erected by Messrs. Burn & Co., and entered in January, 1838.

Dr. Duff returned to Calcutta in 1840, rejoicing in the thought that his labors had resulted in a permanent abode for his school.

The number of pupils (increased to 870 in the beginning of the following session), and the character of the education given, have kept up at the high point then attained, and sometimes far exceeded it. There have been during the last 45 years upwards of 1,000 pupils on an average on the rolls of the Institution every year ; and even as many as 1,000 sometimes present. But Dr. Duff was mistaken in thinking that now the Institution had got a permanent residence. For on the disruption taking place in the Church of Scotland in 1843, all her missionaries in India, as elsewhere, felt compelled to leave the Established Church, the building into which they had so lately entered, as also the valuable library and philosophical apparatus collected by Dr. Duff at great trouble and expense. Teachers, pupils, and converts, followed them in search of new accommodation. On the 16th January, 1844, the examination of the Institution took place for the last time in Cornwallis Square ; at the close, it was intimated that the next session would open on the 4th March, although the missionaries then knew not *where* they should meet. By that day the best, perhaps the largest, and certainly the most commodious native house in Calcutta, (68, Nimtolla Street) now the Jute godown of Messrs. Ralli and Mavrojani, was repaired and occupied ; a library of upwards of 1,000 volumes formed ; and a new site, that on which the present building stands, purchased for the sum of Rs. 18,000. Upwards of 700 boys were present in the new house within a few days after its opening. Before the close of the Session 1,257 boys were enrolled, of whom 115 were in the College Department.

The present premises, also built by Messrs. Burn & Co., were not however completed till March 1857. They cost £15,000, which were raised by Dr. Duff in nearly equal proportions from friends in Scotland, England, and America. The building is, as regards plan and structure, most suitable. It consists of an extensive frontage facing the street, with a grand central portico of six doric columns, and two advanced wings also faced with columns. In the north wing, on the third story, is the library, containing some 7,000 volumes, three or four oil paintings of Drs. Duff, Ewart, and Smith, and a marble bust of Dr. Duff. In the second story in the same wing is a double gallery, capable of containing 400 pupils, and at the back of the building is a large hall, surrounded on three sides with galleries, the whole capable of containing 750 pupils. There are in the Institution altogether 28 class rooms (besides these two halls and galleries, an examination hall, and a laboratory) intended to accommodate from 1,000 to 1,200 boys.

There are two other houses of much public interest, whose

history is closely connected with the history of the Free Church Institution; and these are 22 Mirzapore Street, lately occupied by the Cathedral Mission College, and 2 Cornwallis Square. In both of them Dr. Duff lived for a long time. The first of them was his dwelling-house during part of his earliest stay in Calcutta. In it were delivered those famous lectures on the evidences of Christianity which issued in the conversion of the Rev. K. M. Bannerjea, LL. D., late Professor of Bishop's College, but who was at the time editor of the *Inquirer* newspaper. In the other house, built for the Mission, he lived during his latter stay in Calcutta.

THE FREE CHURCH ORPHANAGE, BOARDING-SCHOOL AND NORMAL SCHOOL.

(32/6, *Beadon Street.*)

The first of these was opened in 1843 with five pupils, a number which soon increased to 36.

In July 1874, the three schools removed into the present imposing building, 32/6, Beadon Street, the foundation stone of which was laid with speech and ceremony by the Lieutenant-Governor, Sir George Campbell. It has cost altogether a lakh of rupees, and is intended for a dwelling-house for two Missionaries with their families, and a home for the Zenana Teachers of the Mission, as well as for the teachers, orphans, and boarders of the schools. The schools were formerly located in Camac Street, in 159, (then 123) Boitakhana, or Bow Bazar Street, and in 14, Canal Street, Entally. The present number of pupils is 90.

The Free Church Orphanage is intended to give a useful unsectarian Christian education to the daughters of native christians of all denominations, and to such orphan girls of heathen parentage as may be brought to it.

DR. DUFF'S HINDU GIRLS' SCHOOL.

(*133, Manicktollah Street.*)

In May, 1857, Dr. Duff opened this school for the instruction of Hindu girls of the better classes, in a Brahmin's house in Nimtolla, rented to him for the purpose by its proprietor, at the expense of much persecution from his countrymen. In spite of the general apathy in regard to female education, and the bitter hostility of many, the school prospered. In 1858 it removed to 167, Manicktollah Street; and in 1863, Dr. Duff, shortly before leaving India for good, bought the house in which the school is at present, from funds which had been placed at his disposal, and after putting it into a state of thorough repair, presented it to the Free Church Mission.

Since 1858 the school has been under the superintendence of Mrs. Chatterjea, herself a convert of the Mission, and the wife of Professor U. C. Chatterjea, of the Free Church College. The number of pupils is about 100.

THE GENERAL ASSEMBLY'S INSTITUTION.

(*Cornwallis Square.*)

This Institution was established in 1830 by the General Assembly of the Church of Scotland. It is the oldest Institution of the kind in India; for it was here that the system, now all but universal, was first introduced,—the system of imparting the highest forms of knowledge, including sound Christian instruction, through the medium of the *English* language, instead of Bengali or Sanskrit which had previously been exclusively favoured by the Government, by Oriental scholars, and even by Missionaries themselves.

This system was introduced by Dr. Duff, who began his missionary labours by founding the General Assembly's Institution. Valuable help in the way of procuring pupils was given by the celebrated Rajah Ram Mohun Roy. The success of the Institution soon surpassed all expectations. The Governor General declared publicly that it had produced "unparallelled results."

For several years after its establishment, the Institution was carried on in various hired premises. But on the 23rd February, 1837, the foundation stone of the present building in Cornwallis Square, was laid by David Macfarlan, Esq., Chief Magistrate of Calcutta. The new building was completed, and began to be occupied in 1838,—a large and handsome building of one story, of a modified Ionic style of architecture, surrounded by an extensive garden compound in which there is also a Mission-house. The situation is perhaps the best that could have been selected, being at the side of a spacious and airy square, and in the very centre of the Hindoo population. In 1879, in consequence of a great increase in the number of students, it became necessary to provide enlarged accommodation. This was done by building a range of class-rooms along the front of the original block. A suite of rooms for the missionaries was also added in a second story over the new class-room. The cost of these additions was upwards of

Rs. 50,000, and was entirely defrayed from the surplus fees of the Institution.

The Institution was temporarily closed in 1844, in consequence of the Missionaries having joined the Free Church. But it was re-opened in 1846 by the Church of Scotland, under the superintendence of the late Rev. Dr. Ogilvie, by whom it was carried on uninterruptedly and with great efficiency till his death in 1871.

The College Department was affiliated to the University of Calcutta in 1864, and at the same time obtained a Grant-in-aid from the Government, of Rs. 350 a month. In 1881, in consequence of the increase in the number of students referred to above, this was raised to Rs. 600 a month.

From the Statistical Returns to Government for 1881 the following facts are taken :—In March, the whole number of students enrolled in five College classes was 501, being the largest number enrolled in any Indian College. The annual cost to Government of educating each student was Rs. 12-8. The fees for the year ending 31st March amounted in the College Department to Rs. 18,365. At the University Examinations of 1880-81, there passsed from this Institution, at the Entrance Examination, 24 candidates; at the First Examination in Arts, 57; at the B.A. Examination, 18; and at the M.A. Honours Examination, 2.

The General Assembly's Institution is divided into two Departments—the College Department and the School Department.

The College Department is divided into five classes. The Students pay a monthly fee of Rs. 5 each. In these classes the regular subjects of the University curriculum are taught, embracing the English language and literature, the Sanskrit Language and Literature, History, Mathematics, pure and applied, Philosophy, and the Doctrines and Evidences of the Christian religion.

The School Department is attended by nearly 800 pupils, divided into 12 classes. Instruction is given in English, Bengali, Sanskrit, History, Geography, Arithmetic, Algebra, and Geometry, according to the degree of advancement of the different classes. Careful attention is given also to instruction in religious knowledge. The pupils in the school pay fees varying in the different classes from 8 annas to Rs. 2-8 a month.

In connection with the General Assembly's Mission, there is a small chapel for bazaar preaching, advantageously situated at the south-west corner of Cornwallis Square. It is used by vernacular preachers of all evangelical denominations, as well as by those of the Church of Scotland.

There is also a Chapel for Native Christians, (St. Andrew's Bengali Church) erected in the Circular Road, nearly opposite to the Sealdah Station of the Eastern Bengal Railway.

LONDON MISSIONARY SOCIETY'S INSTITUTION.

This Institution was founded by the London Missionary Society in the year 1838. The large and handsome building now used, consisting of a library, a hall, and sixteen class rooms, was opened in 1854.

The Institution is divided into three Departments, *viz.*, a College Department for Under-Graduates of the University, a School Department, and a Theological Class for training Christian Natives for missionary work.

The course of study comprises English, Sanskrit, and Bengali Literature, Mental and Moral Philosophy, Mathematics, History and Geography, together with the Sacred Scriptures and Christian Evidences.

The number of Students and Scholars amounts to more than 800.

In connection with the Institution are eight Girl's schools in and near Bhowanipore, and a School and Orphanage at Kourapukur, a village about 6 miles south of Calcutta. There is also a Medical Zenana Mission under the charge of Miss McMicking.

ST. XAVIER'S COLLEGE,

(10 & 11, Park Street,)

Was instituted by the Fathers of the "Society of Jesus," who, in 1834, were sent by His Holiness to support the cause of religion in Calcutta. It owed its first establishment to the pious generosity of two rich residents, one of whom vacated, and gave up his own house for the purpose, and the other furnished the College throughout, and bestowed a liberal pension for its support during the first few months of its existence.

In the year 1844, the fine building at present occupied by the College, and originally built for the Sans Souci Theatre, in Park Street, was in the market, and was purchased by the Right Rev. Dr. Carew for the sum of Rs. 40,000, (it was then called St. John's College) and on the arrival of the Belgian Jesuits, in 1859, was placed under their efficient management. The building has been improved and extended from time to time, and the house, No 10, Park Street, has been added to the accommodation. The Institution has now on its rolls 480 scholars, of whom 120 are boarders.

The Principal of the College is the Rev. Fr. Lafont, a gentleman of great scientific acquirements, whose labors in diffusing useful scientific knowledge, in a popular form, are not confined to the College, of which he is the distinguished head. He is assisted by an able staff of professors and teachers. The College was affiliated to the University of Calcutta in January 1862.

Besides the Meteorological Observatory erected in the College premises, the Rev. Fr. Lafont has exerted himself in establishing the first Spectroscopic Observatory in India, at a cost of Rs. 20,000, the Government of Bengal aiding with a handsome donation of Rs. 7,000.

The discipline and training, mental and moral, pursued in the College, are well-known and appreciated.

LORETTO HOUSE.

(7, Middleton Row, Chowringhee.)

Established in 1842, and placed under the care of the Loretto Sisters. The Institution is principally intended for young ladies of the better classes of society, and is highly esteemed for its liberal education and good discipline.

CATHEDRAL FEMALE SCHOOL,
BOW BAZAAR FEMALE SCHOOL,
ST. JOHN'S FEMALE SCHOOL,

Are branch Institutions, under the care of the same Loretto Sisters, and designed for the girls of the middle and lower classes, many even receiving education gratis.

They were established in 1842, 1844, and 1868, and number upwards of 400 pupils.

THE CATHEDRAL ORPHANAGE,

Established 1844, managed by the Christian Brothers. The object of the Institution is to afford shelter and education to the homeless and fatherless poor of the city. Since the time of Dr. Carew, many additions have been made to the building by His Grace Dr. Steins, to accommodate the continually increasing number of orphans. The Orphanage has now its full complement of 220. Some few pay or are paid for by Government and friends.

ST. JOSEPH'S SCHOOL,

(69, Bow-Bazaar,)

Formerly the Bow-Bazaar Boy's school; likewise conducted by the Christian Brothers, supplies a want long felt by the Catholics of Calcutta—a cheap boarding-school for the poor. It has both a paying and a free department. The pupils number over 300, including 80 boarders. Established in 1844.

ENTALLY ORPHANAGE,

Under the care of the Loretto Sisters. The spacious buildings and extensive grounds situtated in North Road, Entally, were purchased very cheap, by Dr. Carew in 1844, for a female orphanage. Boarders of three classes are admitted; Pupils who pay, Christian orphans who receive a free education, and Native orphan converts. Each division is strictly separated from the other. There are at present 40 Boarders, 225 Christian orphans, 50 Native converts.

THE CALCUTTA FREE SCHOOL,

(Free School Street,)

Is a noble Institution, in which indigent Christian children of both sexes are taught, clothed, fed, and trained for future life. It was founded in the year 1799, by the union of the funds of the "Old Calcutta Charity," and the "Free School Society," which then amounted to over three lakhs of Rupees, or £30,000. A garden house in Jaun Bazaar was purchased for Rs. 28,000. A large amount was added by subscriptions, and a monthly grant also was made by Government. In 1796, a new school for the girls was erected. In 1830, Bishop Turner suggested the expediency of placing the school under Clerical Superintendence, and the Free School Church was erected. It was consecrated by Bishop Wilson, in February 1833. The present spacious buildings were erected in 1854, after the collapse of the old building, which had been undermined by jackals.

ST. JAMES' SCHOOL,

(84, Lower Circular Road,)

Was opened in March 1864. It occupies a commodious building adjoining St. James' Church. It is designed for the children of parents having only a moderate income, too small to enable them to pay the charges of the existing schools, and too large to allow of their being considered as destitute persons, entitled to gain free admission for their children upon the foundations of La Martiniere or the Free

School. The building was originally intended to accommodate 60 Boarders and 50 Day Scholars; but through the energetic efforts of the Chaplain of St. James', it was enlarged in 1870, and now affords accommodation for 200 boarders and day scholars, who receive a good, solid and useful education.

PRATT MEMORIAL GIRLS' SCHOOL,

(84a, Lower Circular Road, 24-Pergunnah's side.)

THE MILITARY ORPHAN INSTITUTION.

This Institution was founded in the year 1782, by the generous and comprehensive mind of Colonel Kirkpatrick, and was first located at Howrah; but about 1790, it was removed to the fine premises now occupied at Kidderpore. Its objects are to educate and settle in life destitute orphans of officers and soldiers on the Bengal establishment.

The Institution supports two schools—one for the daughters of deceased officers, called the Upper School, and occupying the extensive building at Kidderpore; the other for the daughters of European privates and Non-commissioned officers, and at present located in the House No. 86 in the Lower Circular Road.

EUROPEAN FEMALE ORPHAN ASYLUM,

(58, Lower Circular Road, Town side.)

The objects of this Institution are the protection and bringing up of Female Orphans of pure European parentage, giving them a sound and useful Christian education, and sending them out, at fit ages, as Nursery Governesses or domestic servants. It owes its origin to Mrs. Thomson, wife of the Rev. T. Thomson, who began it in July 1815. It was originally intended for the orphans of soldiers; but it now offers a home for the orphan children of European settlers, Railway employés, Tradesmen's Assistants, Policemen, &c.

There are between 50 and 60 girls in the school. The annual expenditure is about Rs. 16,000; of which Rs. 8000 is derived from Government and funded property, and the remainder from subscriptions and donations. It is managed by a Committee of Ladies.

THE BETHUNE NATIVE FEMALE SCHOOL.

(Cornwallis Square.)

This school was established by the late Hon'ble J. E. D. Bethune, for the education of the daughters of Native Gentlemen, and was the first school of the kind in Calcutta. The foundation stone of the handsome building which it occupies was laid with great *eclât*, in November 1850, by the Hon'ble Sir John Littler, then Deputy Governor of Bengal. The buildings are spacious and admirably adapted for the purpose for which they were designed, and there is a fine residence for the Head Mistress; but although it has been fostered and largely aided by Government, and large promises of support were made by some of the leading Natives, and the Schooling fees are merely nominal, it has had but a languishing existence.

SEAL'S FREE COLLEGE.

(1, Sunker Ghose's Lane, Thunthunnea.)

Established under the patronage of Baboo Heera Lall Seal and Brothers.

NORMAL AND CENTRAL SCHOOLS AND ZENANA MISSION.

(21, Cornwallis Square.)

THE USEFUL ARTS SCHOOL.

(77, Dhurrumtollah Street.)

Established 1860. Principal, Rev. C. H. A. DALL, M. A. There are about 230 pupils, receiving a plain education in Bengali, Sanskrit, and English.

CALCUTTA "RAGGED," OR ROVERS' SCHOOL.

(Old Baitakhannah Bazaar Road.)

One hundred homeless and orphan boys are taught the Rudiments of Knowledge and various Industries.

ST. STEPHEN'S GOVERNMENT AIDED PAROCHIAL SCHOOL.

(Hastings.)

ARMENIAN PHILANTHROPIC ACADEMY.

(16, Loudon Street.)

THE ORIENTAL SEMINARY.

(336, Chitpore Road.)

Established by the late Baboo Gour Mohun Addy.

THE BENEVOLENT INSTTUTION,

(43, *Bow Bazaar.*)

This School was founded in 1809, for the instruction of indigent Christian children.

THE SCHOOL OF ART,

(*125, Baitakhannah Street.*)

The Calcutta School of Industrial Art was founded in 1854, by an Association of gentlemen under the name of The Society for the promotion of Industrial Art," which "originated at a meeting held at the house of Mr. Hodgson Pratt in the early part of that year. The object of the Society was stated to be to form schools for East Indian and Native Students for instruction in

First.—Elementary Drawing, Drawing from Models and Natural Objects, and Architectural Drawing.

Secondly.—Etching and Engraving in Wood, Metal and Stone.

Thirdly.—Modelling, including Pottery.

The School was placed under the charge of Mons. Riego, "a French plaster-caste maker," and for some time the internal decoration of buildings in plaster formed the chief occupation of the pupils. A specimen of their work may be seen in the Bengal Legislative Council-room. Early in 1860 Mr. Garrick was appointed master, and a teacher of Wood Engraving was also employed.

In 1864, the charge of the School was assumed by the Bengal Government. Mr. Locke, a gentlemen, experienced in Art as a profession, and in the management of Art Schools in England, was appointed Principal, and a systematic course of instruction in what may be termed the practical branches of the Fine Arts was inaugurated. Subsequently a teacher of Lithography was engaged, and the curriculum of the School now comprises—Free-hand drawing, Engineering drawing, Colouring, Drawing on stone, Wood engraving, &c.

There are now 140 pupils on the rolls.

Some works of Art of a high class have been executed at the School, amongst which may be noticed the Original Drawings for Dr. Fayrer's Thanatophidiæ, and the Illustrations for Baboo Rajendralala Mitra's work on the Antiquities of Orissa.

The pupils pay an entrance fee and a small monthly schooling fee.

LITERARY AND SCIENTIFIC SOCIETIES, &c.

THE ASIATIC SOCIETY.

The Asiatic Society of Bengal, one of the oldest Institutions of its kind, was founded by Sir William Jones, then Chief Justice of Bengal, on the 15th January, 1784. Warren Hastings, the then Governor, became its first patron. "The bounds of its investigations," says the illustrious founder in his first discourse, "will be the geographical limits of Asia, and within these limits its inquiries will be extended to whatever is performed by man or produced by nature."

The monthly meetings, of the Society are held on the first Wednesday of every month, at 9 o'clock P. M., at No. 57, Park Street, when antiquarian and scientific papers are read and discussed. There are about three hundred paying members. The entrance fee is Rs. 32, and Town members pay Rs. 9, and Mofussil members Rs. 6 *per quarter*, for which they receive the publications of the Society and have the use of the large library. The business of the Society is administered by a council chosen annually. The meeting house is the property of the Society. Several additions were made to the original building in 1836 and 1850, to accommodate the increasing library and collections.

Since the foundation of the Society, its literary activity has been uninterrupted. The first publication had the title of "Asiatic Researches." They extend over twenty *quarto* volumes, issued between 1799 and 1839. In 1829, Captain

James D. Herbert commenced to issue, in connection with the Society, a monthly publication, called "Gleanings in Science." He issued three volumes, the last one (vol. III of 1831) being completed by James Prinsep, as Captain Herbert left for Lucknow to join his appointment as astronomer to the King of Oudh. In the beginning of 1832 James Prinsep changed the title of the "Gleanings" to "Journal of the Asiatic Society of Bengal," and continued to be the editor till 1838. The first seven volumes, from 1832 to 1838, contain his numerous essays on Indian Antiquities and Paleography, and his famous readings of the Asoka Inscriptions. On his departure, the Journal became the property of the Society, and from 1839, when the "Asiatic Researches" ceased, bulky annual volumes have been printed. Since 1865, the Proceedings of the Society have been issued separately, whilst the Journal has since then been annually issued in two parts, each consisting of four quarterly numbers, the first part being devoted to Literature Philology, and Antiquities, and the second to Natural History and Science. The Journal and Proceedings contain annually from 800 to 1000 pages.

The Society receives no pecuniary aid from Government. Another department which has greatly added to the renown of this old Society is the "Bibliotheca Indica." In 1838, the Honorable Court of Directors gave the Society a monthly grant of Rs. 500, for the printing of Oriental works, and since that time the Society has issued, under the above title, over five hundred fasciculi of numerous Sanskrit, Arabic, Persian, Pali, and Hindi works, both in original and in translation, among them a fine collection of Indian historians. This monthly grant was continued, in 1858, by the Imperial Government, and was lately increased by Rs. 250 per mensem, exclusively to be devoted to Sanskrit, the addition being a portion of the Sanskrit allotment to Rs. 6000 per annum, allowed by Government for the classification, copying, and purchase of Sanskrit Manuscripts in Bengal.

The Museum of the Society, up to 1866, contained a large collection of Zoological and Ethnological specimens, besides many Archæological reliefs and statues of great value, nearly all of which were presents made to the Society by its members. The Society, unable to provide space and funds for the maintenance of its ever increasing collections, offered, in 1865, the museum to Government, on condition that the Society was to receive *in perpetuo* free quarters in the new Imperial Museum, in Chowringhee, the building of which was about to be commenced. Government accepted this, and the transfer of the Society's Museum, under that condition, was legalised by Act XVII of 1866.

The Society has, however, retained its rich collection of coins, copper *sanads*, portraits and pictures, busts, and its large library.

The Library contains above fifteen thousand volumes; among them more than five thousand Sanskrit, Arabic, Persian and Hindustani Manuscripts. There is also a fine collection of Burmese and Nepalese Manuscripts. The greater portion of the Manuscripts belonged formerly to the old College of Fort William. The bulk of the Arabic and Persian Manuscripts formed part of Tippú Sultán's library, and had been transferred from Seringapatam to the College of Fort William (1804). When the college was reduced, the Honorable Court of Directors presented the greater part of the library to the Society. Among the Manuscripts there are many *chief d'œuvres* of caligraphy and oriental painting.

The collection of portraits, busts and paintings is well worth a visit.

The rooms of the Society are daily open to members from 10 to 5 o'clock, Sundays and holidays excepted. Strangers may visit the library and inspect the coins on application to the Honorary Secretaries.

THE INDIAN MUSEUM.

(27, Chowringhee Road.)

In the year 1866, an Act was passed by the Governor-General of India in Council providing for the establishment of a Public Museum in Calcutta, "to be devoted in part to collections illustrative of Indian Archæology and of the several branches of Natural History, and in part to the preservation and exhibition of other objects of interest, whether historical or physical, in part to the records and offices of the Geological Survey of India, and in part to the fit accommodation of the Asiatic Society of Bengal, and to the reception of their Library, Manuscripts, Maps, Coins, Busts, Pictures, Engravings and other property." The Act provided for the erection of a building for this purpose, to be completed within five years from the date of the passing of the Act; and constituted a body of trustees. It also provided that all expenses and salaries, connected with the Indian Museum, should be defrayed by the Government of India.

As has been stated, the Act of 1866 provided that the Asiatic Society should be accommodated in the new building, but in 1876, when the extent of the collections had been more maturely considered, along with some changes which it was found desirable to make in the constitution of the governing body, the Government arranged with the Asiatic Society that for a pecuniary consideration it should relinquish its claim to accommodation in the new building, and hence certain clauses of the Act of 1866 became obsolete and a new Act was passed and received the formal assent of the Governor-General on the 17th December, 1876.

The building was not ready for occupation till 1875, and it is only now becoming gradually completed in its internal fittings. It was erected from the designs of Mr. Walter B. Granville, late Government architect, and has cost £140,000.

It presents a frontage of 300 feet to the Chowringhee Road, with a depth of 270 feet facing Sudder Street. The façade has two stories of great height, in the Italian style of architecture, the two projecting wings and the grand central portico having elegant Corinthian columns. A handsome flight of steps within the portico leads to a lobby, opening on either side into a room 80 by 30. Three fine archways lead to the grand staircase, which is of magnificent proportions, and ascends to the right and left. There is a fine central quadrangle, 180 feet by 105 feet, surrounded by a colonnade, and a rich selection of tropical plants. The columns of the ground floor are in the Roman Doric style; those on the first floor, the Roman Ionic. Around this quadrangle, above and below, are the rooms devoted to the various branches of the Museum. The grand hall at the head of the staircase, over the portico, 59 feet long by 50 feet wide, and 50 feet high, with a fine panelled ceiling, is at present the library. At each of the four corners of the building is a pavilion, 44 feet by 40, in two stories, another incompleted pavilion exists on the two front corners, and will ultimately be surmounted by a high-pitched mansard roof, as will also be the library room over the central portico. The upper exhibition galleries are all lighted from the side roof by an ingenious contrivance which leaves the whole wall space available, and diffuses a soft and equal light through the room.

The Indian Museum building, as already stated, accommodates not only the Natural History, Archæological and Ethnological collections, which were made over by the Asiatic Society to Government, but also the Geological Survey, its offices and Palæontological and Mineralogical collections.

The Geological Survey occupies the north and north-west wings containing two north galleries, each 160 by 40 feet; two corner or pavilion rooms, two west galleries, each 80 by 30 feet; and a series of office rooms, the rest of the building being devoted to the Indian Museum proper.

The Museum is open to the public daily, Sunday inclusive, excepting on Friday in each week, and from the 1st to the 15th May, and from the 1st to the 15th November in each year.

The hours during which the Museum is open to visitors are from 10 A.M. to 5 P.M. from the 1st February to the 1st November, and from 10 A.M. to 4 P.M. from the 16th November to the 31st January.

On entering the lobby to the right, is the entrance to the Archæological galleries and opposite to it is the door leading into the ground series of the Geological Survey collections. We commence with the Archæological Section.

The Archæological galleries are four in number, *en suite*, occupying the south-western wing, and two southern galleries on the ground floor. The first gallery, 80 by 30 feet contains a gateway and a considerable portion of the railing of the famous stupa of Bharhut, described by General Cunningham in his work entitled "Stupa of Bharhut," and a series of casts of the friezes of the rock cut temples of Orissa, and some other sculptures of the Asoka period, all of these sculptures and the originals of the casts dating from about 250, B. C.

The Great Stupa of Bharhut, discovered by General Cunningham in 1873, is rather more than half-way between Allahabad and Jabalpur, and within nine miles of the railway station of Sutna.

The pillars, cross bars and architrave of the railing are richly covered with sculptures, chiefly representing *Jatakas* or scenes in the previous births, of Sakhya Sinha or Gutama, many of which have been transplanted into Western Folklore and fables. Nearly all are accompanied by inscriptions in ancient Pali describing the scenes represented, which adds immensely to the value of the Bharhut railing as a record of Buddhist history. Apart from this fact, however, the sculptures are also noteworthy, not only as illustrating indigenous Indian Art of the date to which they belong, but also as giving delineations of the dress, weapons, technical instruments, furniture and buildings of the period, and in some instances moreover illustrating the domestic life of the people of that day.

The friezes of rock cut temples of Orissa which would

appear to be about the same age as the Bharhut Stupa have been described by Dr. Mitra, and more recently by Messrs. Fergusson and Burgess in their work on the Cave Temples of India.

Besides them there are two colossal human figures from Patna, the ancient Pataliputra of the Greeks; a capital from Mathura, and some casts from the Sanchi Tope.

In the adjoining room is to be found a portion of the architrave and a cast of a pillar from the Asoká railing at the famous temple of Buddha Gaya, where Gutama attained Buddhahood. In the middle of this room are ten bases of capitals from Mathura of especial value from the circumstance that on some of them are recorded the names of Kings by which their age can be approximately determined, and which is about the first century, A.D. Surrounded by the pillars and occupying the centre of the room is a sculpture discovered at Mathura in 1836, by Colonel Stacy. It is carved on both sides with a Bachanalian group. The principal figure has been supposed to represent Silenus, but is considered by General Cunningham probably to be the Scythian Hercules, while on the other hand Mr. Growse believes it to be a representation of the wine-bibbing Balarama, one of the tutelary divinities of Mathura, attended by his wife Revati and the other members of his family.

Among other sculptures from the same locality may be noticed the pillar of a Buddhist railing, and a large figure of Buddha.

In front of the south window of this room stands a huge statue of Buddha with an inscription on the pedestal from the ancient Sravasti, or Sahet Mahet, where Buddha resided during many years of his life, and which was the scene of many of the incidents in the career of the great teacher.

To the right of the entrance to the west gallery is a beautiful slab of marble from the Tope of Amravati representing the dream of Maya, the mother of Buddha, on the night of her conception. The slab was figured by Foucaux in his History of Buddhism, and by Fergusson in his great work on Tree and Serpent worship.

In the cases around the walls is a rich series of Buddhist sculptures from the ancient Ghandara, in Yuzufzai, to the north of Peshawar. These sculptures are well worthy of particular study apart from their interest to Buddhist scholars from the undoubted evidence which they manifest of the influence of Greek Art on Indian Sculptures, in the first century of the Christian era.

In the next gallery 160 by 40 feet, the Buddhist sculptures are arranged geographically in recesses; on the right side, on handsome platforms of artificial stone supported on Asoka pillars, whilst the Brahmanical sculptures are similarly arranged to the left. Down the middle of this long gallery runs a double platform of artificial stone on which are displayed a very extensive series of Plaster of Paris casts of the sculptures occuring on the Hindu temples of Orissa, and which have been described by Dr. Mitra in his great work on the Antiquities of that province.

Amongst the Buddhist Archæological treasures the most noteworthy are those from Sarnath near Benares, the monastery where Buddha taught the benign system of which he was the immortal founder. One of those slabs represents the birth, temptation, teaching, and death of

Buddha and was figured by Foucaux in his work already mentioned.

Beyond the Sarnath series a number of the recesses are devoted to sculptures of different ages from Buddha Gaya and Bihár, with a few from Java.

On the opposite side of the gallery are the Brahmanical sculptures containing the remains from Kalinjara, Bihar, Gaur, Katak, &c., and a few from Java.

The centres of the majority of the recesses are occupied by glass cases containing smaller antiquities including stone and metal implements, old pottery, &c , while in one are exhibited fragments of precious stones, &c., found associated with the two slabs of stone which were supposed to have marked the spot at Buddha Gaya where Sakhya Sinha attained Mirvana, *i. e.*, extinction, or the highest felicity.

Returning to the eastern end of this gallery, the visitor enters the pavilion room devoted to miscellaneous architecture and to inscriptions, the collection of the latter not being very large, but highly important.

In this gallery are to be seen a few examples of Mahommedan enamelled tiles.

Retracing his steps for a short way, the visitor passes out by the first door to the right into the southern verandah, and turning to his right ascends the narrow staircase at this corner of the building, at the top of which be passes one entrance to the Mammalian Gallery, but continuing his way a little further along the upper southern corridor he enters the Bird Gallery.

This gallery at present contains both stuffed birds and reptiles ; but this arrangement will soon be altered, and the whole of the lower cases of the gallery will be devoted only to birds, the reptiles being removed to the south-east pavilion room, at present set apart for the Superintendent of the Museum. The collection of birds is very extensive, but at present only a small section is exhibited, and the specimens have not been put in order since their removal from the Asiatic Society's rooms. Besides the series to be exhibited to the public, there is an extensive collection of skins of birds, kept specially for study purposes.

The reptile collection of stuffed specimens and skeletons is especially rich in the latter objects, so far as the Chetonia are concerned, but we learn that ultimately the other groups will be equally well illustrated. The two iron galleries in the room are fitted up with wall cases, but in addition they are to be supplied with a line of flat cases along the hand railing, and all of these cabinets are to be devoted to the illustration of the Invertebrata, with the exception of the Mollusca. This latter group is soon to be exhibited in the centre of the gallery in cases which are now being constructed for it. The collection of shells is very extensive, and as far as the species of the Indian seas are concerned is almost unrivalled. In the pavilion room to the west, the stuffed collection of fish is exhibited, but this section also, we understand, is only partially completed as the skeletons of the various markedly different forms have yet to be displayed.

In the room leading off this, is the magnificent collection of alcoholic specimens of Reptiles, Amphibia and Fish not yet thrown open to the public, but the arrangement of which is far advanced.

Leaving the bird gallery and retracing his steps to the door leading to the Mammal gallery already passed, the visitor finds himself in the splendid hall measuring 91 by 44 feet.

A large whale, the smaller species of the Bay of Bengal, is suspended from the roof, and the centre of the room is at present occupied by a fine series of skeletons, among which is the skeleton of a gigantic wild elephant. The walls also display a fine series of horns, the hollow horned ruminants on one side, the solid horned on the other.

The Mammalia are arranged in systematic series beginning with man from the south-east corner of the gallery onwards to the north-east, and then backwards on the opposite side to the south-corner. Each genus, and in many cases each species is illustrated by its skeleton in addition to stuffed specimens and skulls. This collection of mammals is very extensive and it wlll be observed that a passage runs behind the cases, but shut off from view in front by a white cloth curtain. The duplicate specimens are stored in recesses in this passage, but besides these there is a very extensive collection of skeletons and mammal skins for the use of students.

Passing out of the Mammalian gallery by its northern exit, the door facing the visitor leads into the Entomological room in which all the invertebrate specimens, with the exception of the Mollusca, are at present stored in cabinets. It contains extensive collections of Arthropoda including Insects, Crustacea, Arachnida and Myriapoda, dried and in alcohol. This room is ultimately destined to receive a small Museum illustrative of comparative Anatomy in its fullest sense, and explanatory of the various groups represented in the Natural History Section of the General Museum.

The Ethnographical collection is not yet exhibited to the public. The gallery devoted to this section is on the ground floor to the east, immediately below the Mammalian gallery which it equals in dimensions.

The Library is contained in the hall at the top of the grand staircases, and it can be consulted by applying to the Superintendent of the Museum. It deals almost exclusively with Archæology and Natural History.

The India Museum is presided over by Dr. J. Anderson, F. R. S., its first Superintendent, assisted by a Deputy Superintendent, Mr. James Wood-Mason; a First Assistant to the Superintendent, Mr. Geoffrey Nevill; a second Assistant, Mr. O. L. Fraser; and a Librarian, Mr. C. H. Dreyer.

THE GEOLOGICAL SURVEY.

The GEOLOGICAL SURVEY OF INDIA first assumed any systematic existence in 1856. For years previously there had been a geologist engaged under the Government in the examination of various parts of the country. But these districts were unconnected, and often at great distances one from the other, so that no attempt could be made at a general or systematic survey. Since 1856, and with slightly increased numbers, steady and continuous progress has been made, and a very large area of the country has been carefully gone over and mapped. For this purpose, the maps prepared by the Topographical and Revenue Surveys, have been taken as the basis on which to record the Geological observations. Every known coal-field has been visited, and most of them mapped and described; many of these have been first made known by the officers of the survey. Eighteen volumes of "Memoirs" descriptive of various parts of the country, largely illustrated with maps, &c., have been published, while at the same time, the fossils or organic remains brought to-light during the progress of these examinations have been and continue to be illustrated in quarto plates, with descriptive letter press, of which many volumes have appeared. Briefer notices of current work are given in each successive quarter, in the "Records" of the Geological Survey, which have now appeared punctually during fourteen years.

The Geological Survey Offices, and Library, and Collections, which have been for many years preserved in a private house rented for the purpose, were removed in 1875 to the new INDIAN MUSEUM in Chowringhee Road. The Library, an absolutely essential adjunct to the Survey, in this country where works of reference were inaccessible, forms a noble series, second to few in the books bearing on Geology, Palæontology and allied subjects, and specially rich in series of transactions of learned societies, both in Europe and America. The larger portion of this collection has been obtained by exchange of the publications of the Geological Survey with these Societies. The Museum is also remarkably rich. In it are preserved, (and these are especially deserving of a visit from the Geological student), the original and type specimens of the various series, figures, &c., described in the Palæontogia Indica;—the noble series from the Indian Cretaceous rocks of Trichinopoly, perhaps one of the finest collections ever made from one formation limited to a confined area, and which have been illustrated in four large volumes, by Dr. Stoliczka;—the almost equally fine series of Jurrassic fossils from Kachh, of which only the Cephalopoda have as yet been published, forming one volume of 60 plates and more than 250 pages of description (159 species);—the very remarkable series of fossil plants described in part by Oldham and Morris, but chiefly by Dr. Feistmantel from the Gondwana series. Tertiary Crabs, from Sind, and the beautiful remains of Amphibia from the Trias bed of the Ranigunj district, described by Professor Huxley, also the fine collection of Siwalik Vertibrata now being described by Mr. Lyddekker, are all preserved in the Museum, and will amply repay careful study. A large series of Indian rocks, minerals, &c., is also exhibited; and among other interesting specimens, blocks of syenitic granites, polished, furrowed, and scored by ice-action, establishing the existence, in these tropical regions, of climatal conditions sufficiently extreme to produce extensive areas of ground-ice at a geological period not more recent than the older Permian of Europe. The principal aim is of course to make this Museum specially illustrative of Indian Geological structure and history. But in order to carry this out, it is necessary to have also large illustrative series of European organic remains and rocks. The collections of Cephalopoda, Brachiopoda, &c., &c., and of plants, from the various formations of Europe and America, will thus be found large, instructive, and good.

Geological Maps of all districts visited by the Survey are preserved in the office, and can be referred to by those desirous of information.

The Geological Survey of India, begun and for twenty-five years conducted, by T. Oldham, LL.D., is now under the direction of H. B. Medlicott, F. R. S., aided by a staff of 13 geologists and assistants, and in the Palæontological Department, by Dr. O. Feistemantel and Mr. Lyddekker.

Mr. F. R. Mallet, F. G. S. is keeper of the Mineralogical Collections and Chemist to the Survey.

A Manual in three volumes with a general Geological Map of India has lately been published by the Survey.

THE ECONOMIC MUSEUM,

(*12, Hastings Street,*)

Was established by Sir George Campbell in 1873. It contains a collection of specimens of the principal Mineral, and Vegetable products of this country, with samples of native manufacture.

THE AGRICULTURAL AND HORTICULTURAL SOCIETY.

The Agricultural and Horticultural Society, was founded in 1820, by the eminent Baptist Missionary, Dr. Carey. Commencing by small degrees, it has gradually been extending its operations—and now numbers upwards of 500 members resident in various parts of the country, from the Punjab to the Madras and Bombay Presidencies. The Society has published 8 vols. of "Transactions" and 20 vols. of a Journal. In these publications will be found a mass of most valuable practical information and useful reading on the subject of cotton, sugar, indigo, tea, coffee, tobacco, rice, silk, wool, vegetable fibres, cochineal, caoutchouc, lac-dye, Indian fruits, manures, timber trees, topographical accounts of various districts, &c., many of which are treated very extensively and satisfactorily.

Formerly the Society cultivated a garden on a spot of ground forming a portion of the Royal Botanic Garden, for nearly 30 years, and performed, through this medium, good service alike to horticulture and floriculture. The Government having resumed the ground, the Society has formed a garden at Alipore, which is now rendering as good service as its predecessor. Its rooms in the Metcalfe Hall contain a small museum abounding in specimens of woods, oils, dyeing and tanning substances, besides other rare productions of the country. There is also a library which, though not large, embraces many valuable works of a character most useful alike to the new comer and the older resident who may be in pursuit of knowledge connected with the teeming riches of this vast Empire.

In the large hall or meeting-room, there are busts of Dr. Carey, the founder, of Dwarkanath Tagore, and of Dr. Wallich, for many years the Superintendent of the Royal Botanic Garden, a Vice-President, and most zealous member of the Society. Several portraits adorn the walls, among which are those of Sir Edward Ryan, Sir Lawrence Peel Messrs. A. Grote and J. A. Crawford, all successively Presidents of the Society. Also a likeness of General Kyd, first Superintendent of the Royal Botanical Garden.

The affairs of the Society are administered by a President, four Vice-Presidents, and a Secretary, all of whom, togather with 12 ordinary members, constitute the Council. There are also committees of Finance, Garden, and Papers, besides several others to report on staple products submitted for examination. The annual subscription is Rs. 32, and an entrance fee of Rs. 8, in return for which members are entitled to participate in plants from the garden, and in vegetable and flower seeds, (of which there are large annual importations from Europe and America) and in the publications of the Society.

THE CALCUTTA PUBLIC LIBRARY.

The establishment of the Calcutta Public Library was determined upon at a public meeting, held in August 1835. It was opened to the public as a Library of reference and a Circulating Library in March 1836.

The Library consisted, in the first instance, of books presented by private individuals, and of a large collection of valuable works lent by Government from the College of Fort William. The greater portion of these books has since been presented to the Library.

The Library was first located at the residence of Dr. F. P. Strong, Esplanade Row, free of charge. It remained there till the middle of July 1841, when it was removed to the Fort William College building, which accommodated it until its final removal to the Metcalfe Hall in June 1844.

The members of the Library are either proprietors or subscribers. The value of a share in the Library was originally 300 rupees. It was afterwards raised to 400 rupees, and it is now 500 rupees. Shares issued before the end of 1849, are transferable, and those of a subsequent date are a life-interest only, and are not transferable.

The rates of subscription are 6 rupees; 4 rupees; and 2 rupees, monthly.

The Governing body is composed of a council of 15, one of whom is the President and two are Vice-Presidents. The council consists of a Finance Committee, a book Committee, and a House Committee, who control the details of the management.

The Library has all along been self-supporting, and has made from time to time large additions to its stock of books;

but since 1872, there has been a great decline of subscriptions which form the chief support of the Institution. The means for the purchase of books have thus been curtailed, and the usefulness of the Institution has been seriously impaired.

The Library is supplied with all the Official publications of Government, as well as with the Journals and Transactions of most of the Literary and Scientific Societies of Europe, and new publications of an interesting and standard character are added from time to time.

One Mr. Andrews, who had a Circulating Library in Calcutta in 1780, complains (in advertisement) of the loss he has sustained—"owing to gentlemen going away, and in their hurry not recollecting their being subscribers to the Library, or having any books belonging thereto." He adds, that "books are kept too long, and in many cases cuts or leaves are torn out." We fancy, if the truth were known, that the experience of the Calcutta Public Library at the present date would not be found to differ greatly from that of Mr. Andrews a hundred years ago.

THE BETHUNE SOCIETY.

The Bethune Society was established on the 11th December, 1851, to promote among the educated natives of Bengal a taste for literary and scientific pursuits, and to encourage a freer intellectual intercourse than can be accomplished by other means in the existing state of native society. The meetings of the Society are held monthly during the cold season at the Theatre of the Medical College, at which discourses on Literary, Scientific, or Social subjects are delivered. At these meetings many papers of great interest have been read to crowded audiences, some of which have been printed and published, the expense of which is met by a half-yearly subscription of one rupee from each member.

THE NATIONAL INDIAN ASSOCIATION.

(Bengal Branch.)

This Association was established by Miss Carpenter ten years ago, and has for its objects the promotion of social intercourse between the native and European races, the secular education of native ladies, education of girls, the publication of pure Bengali literature, and other cognate subjects. The Association carries on its work in an unostentatious manner; arranging social gatherings of Bengali ladies at the houses of European ladies, as well as evening parties, &c., where European and native gentlemen may meet together. Home education of native ladies is actively carried on, and this department might be usefully developed were more funds forthcoming. Prizes are offered every year for the production of pure works in Bengali that may be useful to Bengali ladies and girls. The Association has at its disposal several scholarships for native girls in Mofussil schools, enabling the holders to complete their studies in a Calcutta school.

EURASIAN AND ANGLO-INDIAN ASSOCIATION.

The objects of this Asociation are the amelioration of the condition of East Indian or Eurasian community and of the descendents of European parents born in India; and to provide a better education for the children of these classes. Except in the latter object mentioned, in the furtherance of which the Association has received considerable extraneous aid, it has not shown much vitality. Government-aided schools are being established in several hill-stations, at which it is hoped that the children will get a more vigorous education than it is possible to obtain in Calcutta, and thus be enabled them to contend on more even terms with their "native" fellow countrymen.

YOUNG MEN'S CHRISTIAN ASSOCIATION.

(23 Chowringhee Road.)

The objects of this Association are similar to those of similar Associations in England and Scotland. It derives its membership principally from the members of the two Scotch Churches.

THE BRITISH INDIAN ASSOCIATION.

(British Indian Street.)

The object of this Association is to promote the improvement and efficiency of the British Indian Government, by memorialising the authorities, here and in England, for the removal of existing, and prevention of proposed, injurious measures, or for the introduction of such measures as may tend to promote the interests of all connected with this country.

The Association, the members of which are exclusively natives, was established in 1851, and has rendered good service by its intelligent criticism of Government measures, and by its powerful representation of the interests of the landed proprietors.

THE CALCUTTA SOCIETY FOR THE PREVENTION OF CRUELTY TO ANIMALS.

This Society was established in March 1862, during the Vice-Royalty of its first Patron and friend Lord Elgin. Its constitution and plans were formed upon the model of the Royal Society of London, the parent and honoured originator of all similar societies throughout the world.

How much of need there has been for the merciful interference of such a Society may be gathered from the fact, that since its establishment the number of convictions for cruelty to animals obtained by its Agents has amounted to above 20,000 exclusive of a great number prosecuted by the police and private persons.

In 1869, the Society, through the aid of its zealous member, Baboo Peary Chand Mittra, and after the customary battling which these reforms have always had to encounter, obtained a distinct Act of the Bengal Legislature for the prevention of cruelty to animals, forming Act I of the Bengal Council of 1869. Among its early friends appear the cherished names of the Rev. Dr. Duff, and the venerable Archdeacon Pratt, its first and much valued President, till the day of his lamented death; the Rev. Edmund Storrow, Macleod Wyllie, Dr. Allen Webb, Dr. Mouat, Major Herbert, Colonel M. Turnbull, and other gentlemen of note who have passed from amongst us.

The Society is under the special patronage of His Excellency the Viceroy and the Lord Bishop.

The present President of the Calcutta Society is the Judge of the High Court of Judicature. Its Honorary Secretary is Baboo Peary Chand Mittra. It is supported partly by public subscriptions, and partly by a moiety of the fines allowed by the Government; but much more than these two sources have yet supplied is needed to carry out all the humane objects the Society has in view, one of the foremost of which is a supply of drinking water for animals traversing our street.

A Memorial Drinking Fountain, in memory of the late Mr. Colesworthy Grant, for several years Secretary of the Society, has recently been erected in Dalhousie Square, East.

CLUBS.

THE BENGAL CLUB.

The Bengal Club was instituted in the beginning of the year 1827. There is no limit to the number of members.

The management of the Club is vested in a President, Vice-President, and seven other Members of Committee, who are elected annually. The number of members at present on the books of the Club exceeds 650. Members are admitted by ballot. All gentlemen received in general society in Calcutta are eligible. The Viceroy; the Commander-in-Chief in India; the Lieutenant-Governors of Bengal, North-Western Provinces, and Punjab, Members of Supreme Executive Council, and the Lord Bishop of Calcutta, are entitled to privileges of members, without ballot, on payment of fees as permanent Members.

There are three classes of permanent Members—Resident, Non-Resident, and Absent. Gentlemen residing in Calcutta or within 20 miles from Government House, are considered residents and pay 25 rupees quarterly; gentlemen residing in India, at a greater distance than 20 miles, are considered non-residents, and pay, if within 100 miles from Calcutta, rupees 12-8 per quarter, if more than 100 miles 25 rupees per year.

Absent members do not pay during their absence. The entrance fee, on election, is 200 rupees.

The accommodation of the Club at present consists of the Club House, No. 33, Chowringee Road, a large house in the same compound, devoted to bed-rooms for members, the houses No. 1, Park Street, and No. 1, Russell Street; divided into chambers for members permanently residing and the large house, No 5, Russell Street, also divided into chambers.

The Club House, No. 33, Chowringhee Road, was the residence of Thomas Babington Macaulay, afterwards Lord Macualay, during his four years' sojourn in India, 1834-38, but has been much altered.

The Bengal Club reciprocates with the Bombay (Byculla) Club, the Madras Club and the Hong-Kong and Shanghai Clubs, admitting the members of those clubs if visiting Calcutta to all the privileges of Honorary Membership for the time. These clubs doing the same with members of the Bengal Club visiting their clubs.

THE UNITED SERVICE CLUB.

(30, 31, Chowringhee, 1, 2, and 3, Kyd Street, and 56 Park Street.)

The Bengal Military Club was instituted in the year 1845. On the 15th March, 1853, its designation was changed to the Bengal United Service Club. The number of Members is unlimited, and consists of Commissioned Officers and Chaplains in Her Majesty's Military and Naval services, and of Members of Her Majesty's Indian Civil Service; also of such Barrister-Judges of the High Court as many have received permanent appointments from the Home Government. The Members are elected by ballot. The Governor-General, Commander-in-Chief, and all ordinary Members of the Executive Council of the Government of India, may be admitted without ballot; also the Chief Justice of the

Calcutta High Court. The concerns of the Club are managed by a Committee, consisting of a President and 12 Members stationed at the Presidency. The entrance fee of each member is fixed at Rs. 100, and, in addition, a fee of 10 rupees as a donation to the Library fund, and a similar sum as donation to the Billiard Fund. The subscription of each member is fixed at 12 rupees per annum, payable in advance, and 3 rupees per mensem in addition for each member resident in Calcutta, and 1 rupee for members stationed in Dum-Dum, Barrackpore or Ishapore. A limited number of rooms are allotted to resident members for permanent occupation, and there is also provision to the extent of the means of accommodation for temporary residents. The Club possesses an excellent Library and Reading-room; and the general accommodation has of late been greatly enlarged and improved. The number of members is over 600.

THE GERMAN CLUB.

(40, Free School Street.)

On occasion of the patriotic dinner (Friedensfein) given by the German Community at the private residence of Mr Eisenlohr, No. 19, Garden Reach Road on February 1871, it was proposed to establish a Musical Club with the object of fostering German Music and the Social Life of the German element of Calcutta.

Accordingly, the German Musical Society was established at No. 5, Hare Street, Mr. Drescher (since deceased) having been entrusted with the Musical Leadership.

In consequence of the great success of this experiment it was resolved at a General Meeting, held on the 12th

March 1872, to establish the German Club, in which the practice of music should continue to be a feature.

On the 2nd April, 1872, the German Club was inaugurated in its present situation, No. 40, Free School Street.

Its chief object is—

"To offer to the German Community of Calcutta a place of recreation, where German Music, Gymnastics, German Theatricals and the Amenities of Social Life," amongst the members of the Club, will be promoted.

Mr. F. W. Stutz was the first president, and on his departure from Calcutta, Mr. F. Eisenlohr was elected to the chair. The Musical Leadership, after the decease of Mr. Ignace Drescher, was conferred on Herr Stoeckel.

HOSPITALS AND CHARITABLE INSTITUTIONS.

THE MEDICAL COLLEGE HOSPITAL.

(College Street.)

This splendid building was erected from funds obtained from the Old and New Fever Hospitals, balance of the Funds of the Lottery Committee, and a donation of Rs. 50,000 from Rajah Pertaub Chunder Singh. The building was designed and erected by Messrs. Burn & Co., of this city. The foundation stone was laid on the 30th September, 1848, by the Marquis of Dalhousie with Masonic Ceremonies, and the building was opened for the reception of the sick on the 1st December, 1852.

The style of architecture is the Corinthian, and it is capable of accommodating about 300 sick people. It is a lofty structure and contains a handsome Operating Theatre and Council Room.

The Eye Infirmary is in Halliday Street. Here aid is given to an average of about 600 in, and 6000 out-patients annually.

The present Hospital has been found for some years to be too small for the number of patients seeking admission, and a new ward is being constructed to the S.-W., for obsteric cases, the present Hospital being reserved for surgical cases only on its completion. The new ward is a three-storied building consisting of a central block for the wards, and four wings at each corner, connected with the main building by a short passage, in which are situated the Delivery Room, Latrines, &c. The Ward when completed will probably be the most perfect Hospital in the world, it having been designed according to the latest and most approved rules of medical science. The extension works include, besides the above mentioned ward, quarters for the Hospital Nurses, and a ward for Contagious Diseases.

PRESIDENCY GENERAL HOSPITAL.

(South of the Maidan.)

The premises now denominated the General Hospital were, in their original state, occupied as a garden house by an individual from whom they were purchased by Government in 1768. They have been from time to time enlarged, and now afford ample accommodation, in separate buildings, for patients and for the Medical officers and establishment attached to the Institution. The situation of the Hospital is airy and healthy.

It is open to Seamen and Europeans of all classes. A charge of one rupee per diem is made for private accommodation.

THE MILITARY HOSPITAL.

(South of the Race Course.)

This fine building, formerly occupied by the Sudder Court, and which was originally erected for a Hospital, is now devoted to its legitimate purpose.

THE MAYO HOSPITAL.

(Strand Road, North.)

So long ago as the year 1793, a Hospital was established

by the Marquis Cornwallis, in the Fouzdaree House, Chitpore Road, for the relief of "the native inhabitants of Calcutta generally, and more particularly for the labouring part of them." In 1796, the Hospital was removed to premises in Dhurrumtollah Street. Subscriptions to the amount of 54,000 rupees were raised, and a monthly allowance of 600 rupees was granted by Government. In 1810, further contributions were given, and the Government allowance was increased to 1,000 rupees per mensem; this was subsequently increased to 2,000 rupees. The Institution pursued an uninterrupted career of usefulness until the year 1871, when a proposal was made to remove it to a more salubrious situation on the banks of the river, above the Mint. The question was warmly discussed, but ultimately the proposal was carried. A portion of the Dhurrumtollah property was sold for 80,000 rupees. The Gurunhatta Dispensary, attached to the Hospital, fetched Rs. 16,000; Rs. 78,990 were raised by subscription; Rs. 10,000 were left by Mr. DaSouza for building purposes, and the surplus of the Mayo Memorial Fund, Rs. 50,000 was transferred to the Hospital, so that without touching the funded property of the Hospital, amounting to about 3 lakhs of rupees, the Governors were able to meet the expenses connected with a new building. The new Hospital was designed by Mr. A. T. Osmond; Messrs. Mackintosh, Burn & Co. were the contractors; and the cost of erection was Rs. 2,46,694. The foundation stone was laid by His Excellency the Viceroy, on the 3rd February 1873, and the building was opened on the 5th September 1874.

The building has two stories and gives accommodation

for about 120 patients, with out-patients' rooms, and quarters for the Resident Medical officers.

A portion of the old Hospital premises in Dhurrumtollah was retained for an out-door Dispensary. There are three other Dispensaries attached to the Hospital—in Chitpore Road, in Colinga, and in Sukea's Lane.

The present sources of income are as follow:—

		Rs.
Government Donation and allowance	...	29,656
Interest of Funded and other Investments	...	12,744
Baretto's Legacy	...	3,062
Tagore's Legacy	...	848
Rupees	...	46,310

The permanent expenditure may be set down at Rs. 48,000 per annum, leaving a deficiency of Rs. 2,000 per annum to be made up by private subscriptions, besides sums necessary for repairs and other extra expenses.

Opposite the Hospital, on the river bank, is the Burning Ghat, in which all Hindus who die in the town are cremated.

THE CAMPBELL SCHOOL.

(Sealdah.)

This building was originally erected for a market, but proving a failure, it was converted into a Pauper Hospital, towards which the Municipality of Calcutta contribute 30,000 rupees a year, the remaining cost being made up by Government. It is still a Pauper Hospital, under a different name, and affords a good field for the study of clinical medicine to native students.

DISTRICT CHARITABLE SOCIETY.

(19/1, Lall Bazar Street.)

This Society was established in the year 1830, under the auspices of Bishop Turner. The funds consist of a monthly donation of Rs. 1200 from Government, of voluntary contributions from private individuals, and of the congregational collections from the various Churches. In addition to these there are the following permanent endowments :—

Lady William Bentinck's Fund, 1835.

Dwarkanath Tagore's Fund for the poor blind, 1838.

Mrs. English's Charity, 1840.

Lokenath Fund for poor invalids, 1854.

Prince Jameeroodeen's Charity, 1856.

Sreemutty Bamasoondaree's Fund, 1865.

Radhamadhub Banerjee's Charity, 1865.

Baboo Chumutkar Krishna Ghose's Fund, 1866.

Baboo Eshan Chunder Bose's Charity, 1867.

The "Cheke" Fund, 1870.

The interest on which forms part of the income of the Society.

An ALMSHOUSE and LEPER ASYLUM, in Amherst Street, are established and maintained from its funds.

ST. VINCENT'S HOME,

(Diamond Harbour Road.)

This Home, destined to offer a shelter to destitute females was founded in 1868. His Grace Dr. Steins, in 1873, established a Magdalen Asylum and placed both institutions under the kind care of the Daughters of the Cross. The Home has an yearly average of 60 inmates.

THE D'SOUZA HOME.

(138, Dhurrumtollah Street.)

This Home was founded in the year 1878 from funds left for the purpose by the late Thomas D'Souza. It provides a home for 10 women and about 20 children. The only qualification required from applicants for admission are that they shall be of Eurasian parentage, and have no means of sustenance.

CALCUTTA SAILORS' HOME.

(13, Strand Road, North.)

The original establishment was opened in 1837 in Bow-Bazaar, in the house now occupied as the Police Magistrate's Court. The house was purchased by Government, and with the funds thus acquired the present imposing looking building was erected. It was opened in January 1868. It is under the management of a Committe, elected annually, and of a Secretary, Superintendent and Deputy Superintendent : other officials carrying out the necessary details.

Its objects is to provide board and lodging for seamen at a reasonable rate, to protect them from extortion and imposition, and to take care of their hard-earned wages until they leave Calcutta. It is conducted on liberal principles, and great attention is paid to the comfort and welfare of the inmates. It is also a refuge for distressed or shipwrecked men. It is capable of accommodating about 250 men and about 20 officers.

Men ashore for a day's liberty, can, at the Home, get a good substantial meal which costs them less than elsewhere. A well conducted bar is opened at proper times, which saves many a poor fellow from losing his money and health in the low dens of iniquity which abound in the city.

PRESIDENCY JAIL.

Average number of Prisoners nearly 1,000, of whom about half are employed in Manufactures, such as cloth and gunny weaving, coir weaving, oil-pressing, foundry work, carpentry, and blacksmith's work.

ALIPORE JAIL.

Average number of Prisoners over 2,000, of whom 1,550 are employed in Manufactures. There is extensive Jute-spinning Machinery attached to this Jail, which employs about 300 convicts; also a Printing and Lithographic department, in which 365 convicts are engaged.

COMMERCIAL.

THE BENGAL CHAMBER OF COMMERCE.

OFFICE—*Bonded Warehouse, 102, Clive Street.*

Secretary—H. W. I. WOOD.

THE BROKERS' EXCHANGE.

OFFICE—*Bonded Warehouse.*

THE CALCUTTA TRADES ASSOCIATION.

OFFICE—*Dalhousie Square.*

Secretary—E. HICKIE.

THE BANK OF BENGAL.

Established 1809.

OFFICE—*3, Strand Road.*

Secretary and Treasurer—R. HARDIE.

AGRA BANK, (LIMITED.)

HEAD OFFICE—*Nicholas Lane, London.*

OFFICE—*26, Mangoe Lane.*

Manager—W. BLACKHALL.

Branches at Edinburgh, Madras, Bombay, Agra, Kurrachee, Lahore, and Shanghai.

CHARTERED MERCANTILE BANK OF INDIA, LONDON AND CHINA.

HEAD OFFICE—*50 Old Broad Street, London.*

CALCUTTA AGENCY—*68, Dalhousie Square.*

Agent—C. H. HERBERT.

Agencies at Bombay, Madras, Colombo, Galle, Kandy,

Singapore, Penang, Batavia, Hong-kong, Shanghai, Foochow, Hankow, and Yokohama.

CHARTERED BANK OF INDIA, AUSTRALIA AND CHINA.

HEAD OFFICE—*Hatton Court, Threadneedle Street, London.*

CALCUTTA AGENCY,—*5, Council House Street.*

Agent—JOHN AIKMAN.

Agencies at Akyab, Bombay, Hankow, Hong-kong, Rangoon, Shanghai, Singapore, Penang, Batavia, and Manilla.

COMPTOIR D'ESCOMPTE DE PARIS.

HEAD OFFICE—*14, Rue Bergère, Paris.*

CALCUTTA AGENCY—*1, Fairlie Place.*

Manager—THOMAS PAYN.

Agencies (in the East) at Bombay, Bourbon, Saigon, Hong-kong, Shanghai, and Yokohama.

DELHI AND LONDON BANK, (LIMITED.)

HEAD OFFICE—*Royal Bank Building, Bishopsgate Street.*

CALCUTTA BRANCH—*4, Council House Street.*

Manager—THOMAS LONGMUIR.

Agencies at Agra, Jubbulpore, Mooltan, Allahabad, Lahore, Nynee Tal, Bareilly, Loodianah, Patna, Benares, Madras, Rawul Pindi, Bombay, Murree, Cawnpore, Meerut, Shahjehanpore, Darjeeling, Simla, Furrackabad, Mirzapore, Umballa, Umritsur, and Melbourne.

NATIONAL BANK OF INDIA, (LIMITED.)

HEAD OFFICE—*80, King William Street, London.*

CALCUTTA OFFICE—3, *Council House Street.*

Manager—J. CAMPBELL.

Branches at Bombay, Hong-kong, and Madras.

HONG-KONG AND SHANGHAI BANKING CORPORATION.

OFFICE—*1, Mangoe Lane.*

Agent—EDWARD MORRISS.

Branches and Agencies at London, Shanghai, Hankow, Foochow, Saigon, Amoy, Swatow, Yokohama, Bombay, Singapore, Batavia, Manilla, Melbourne, and Sydney.

ORIENTAL BANK CORPORATION.

HEAD OFFICE—*Threadneedle Street, London.*

CALCUTTA BRANCH—*1, Clive Street.*

Agent—GEORGE HARPER.

Branch Banks and Agencies at Bombay, Madras, Colombo, Galle, Kandy, Mauritius, Singapore, Hong-kong, Shanghai, Hiogo, Foochow, Pondicherry, Tellicherry, Yokohama, Melbourne, Sydney, and Port Elizabeth.

RAILWAY COMPANIES.

THE EAST INDIA RAILWAY.

CALCUTTA OFFICES—*East India Railway House, Fairlie Place.*

TERMINUS of the Line and Booking Office at Howrah, accessible by the Bridge, which is free of toll to railway passengers.

The line extends from Howrah to Delhi, 954 miles; with an extension from Allahabad to Jubbulpore, where it joins the G. I. P. Railway to Bombay.

THE EASTERN BENGAL RAILWAY.

CALCUTTA TERMINUS AND AGENCY OFFICE—*Sealdah.*

The line extends from Sealdah to Goalundo, 151 miles, at the junction of the Ganges and Brahmapootra, from which place there is steam communication to Dacca and Serajgunj; and where also Passengers usually embark for Sylhet.

The original Terminus of the line was at Kooshtea, which is now reached by a short branch from the main line.

Passengers for Assam and Darjeeling leave the E. B. R. at Damookhdea, from whence there is a steam ferry communicating with the Northern Bengal Railway.

CALCUTTA & SOUTH-EASTERN RAILWAY.

OFFICE AND TERMINUS—*No. 3, Sealdah.*

The line extends from Calcutta to Canning, 28 miles. It was originally constructed by a Company, for the purpose of giving access to a new Port on the Mutlah River, which it was supposed would prove a formidable rival to the Hooghly, on account of its better navigation.

Extensive Mills were erected for the husking of rice, and it was hoped that the facilities offered for the preparation and shipmenf of produce would command much of the trade of the Eastern Districts. But the project proved a failure, and the Railway was ultimately taken over by Government. It is cheaply worked, and the local traffic yields a fair return.

A Branch line to Diamond Harbour on the Rive Hooghly is under construction.

CALCUTTA TRAMWAY.

The lines at present working are:—

I.—Sealdah Station to the Strand, *viâ* Bow Bazar Street, Dalhousie Square, and Hare Street.

II.—Chitpore to the Strand, *viâ* Chitpore Road, joining No. 1 near the Police Court.

III.—Russapugla to Dalhousie Square, *via* Bhowanipore, Chowringhee, Esplanade and Old Court House Street. Lines are also in course of construction through Dhurrumtollah Street, Wellesley Street, Elliot Road, College Street, Cornwallis Street, Strand Road, &c. The whole scheme includes about 45 miles of streets.

*** *For Time Tables and full particulars of all Indian Railways see Newman's "Indian Bradshaw."*

STEAM COMPANIES.

PENINSULAR AND ORIENTAL STEAM NAVIGATION COMPANY.

CALCUTTA AGENCY—*8, Strand Road.*

Superintendent—CAPTAIN C. J. WILKINSON.

Steamers depart from No. 13, Garden Reach, fortnightly, for London, calling at Madras, Galle, Aden, Suez, Port Said, Malta, and Gibraltar.

COMPAGNIE DES MESSAGERIES MARITIMES DE FRANCE.

Calcutta Agent—A. DE GUIGNE, *5, Council House Street.*

Steamers depart from No. 23, Garden Reach, once every four weeks, for Marseilles, calling at Pondicherry, Galle, Aden, Suez, Port Said, Messina, Naples and Genoa.

BRITISH INDIA STEAM NAVIGATION COMPANY.

Managing Agents—MESSRS. MACKINNON, MACKENZIE & CO., *16, Strand Road, North.*

The Steamers of this Company run

To London—Once a month.

To Queensland—Once a month.

To Bombay—Calling at all ports on the coast—weekly.

Constant communication is also kept up between Rangoon, Moulmein, Penang, Singapore, and all the Tenasserim Ports.

ASIATIC STEAM NAVIGATION COMPANY.

Managing Agents—TURNER, MORRISON & CO.,
6, Lyons Range.

The Steamers of this Company run at regular intervals to Rangoon, Singapore, Ceylon, Bombay, and Mauritius.

THE CITY LINE OF STEAMERS.

The Steamers of this Company leave Calcutta for London direct every fortnight:

Agents—GLADSTONE, WYLIE & CO., *101, Clive Street.*

THE "STAR" LINE OF STEAMERS.

The Steamers of this Company leave Calcutta for London calling at Colombo, once a month:

Agents—HOARE, MILLER & CO., *38, Strand Road.*

There are also several other lines of Steamers running at frequent intervals between Calcutta and London. On an average two steamers a week leave Calcutta for London, and more in the early months of the year.

CHINA STEAMERS.

Agents—APCAR & CO., AND JARDINE, SKINNER & CO.

The Steamers sail for Penang, Singapore, and Hong-Kong about the middle of every month.

INDIA GENERAL STEAM NAVIGATION COMPANY, (LIMITED.)

Managing Agents—SCHOENE, KILBURN & CO.,
4, Fairlie Place.

Regular fortnightly River Steamers to Assam and Cachar on alternate Saturdays.

THE RIVERS STEAM NAVIGATION COMPANY, (LIMITED.)

Agents in Calcutta—MACNEILL & CO., *1, Lyon's Range.*

Regular Steamers to Debrughur (Assam) and inter mediate Stations. And a weekly steamer to Chandbally in Orissa.

EXCURSIONS FROM CALCUTTA.

Under this head we propose to notice a few places in the neighbourhood which may be visited in a day's journey. Three lines of Railway, all constructed within the last 25 years, afford facilities to Visitors and Residents desirous to escape the din of the city, and to breathe a purer atmosphere than a great city can supply. And then there is the river—the great highway—through which, still, the bulk of the productions of the country reach Calcutta, the Port of shipment, and the banks of which, from Garden Reach to Chandernagore abound in picturesque beauties. We notice first

THE BOTANICAL GARDEN,

(Seebpore.)

The Royal Botanical Garden (founded in 1786 by the Honorable East India Company, by the advice of General Kyd, of the Bengal Engineers, who became its first Superintendent), is situated in the Suburb of Howrah on the opposite side of the river from Calcutta and immediately below Bishop's College. The upper entrance gate of the garden is about 3¼ miles below the Hooghly Bridge, and is easily reached by a good road which passes through Howrah and the village of Seebpore. The garden can also be conveniently reached by the river either by taking boat at Calcutta or by driving down to the Nemuck Mahal Ghât on the Calcutta side, and there hiring a boat and crossing to the garden which is just opposite. In either case the best landing place is at the river-side ghât which is about the middle of the garden.

The extent of the garden is 272 acres, and it has a river frontage of exactly a mile. Originally intended for visitors on foot only, the garden has by the liberality of Government been recently supplied with excellent driving roads, so that the whole of the grounds may now be gone over without leaving one's carriage. Entering by the Howrah gate, (at the North-West corner of the garden) the visitor is confronted by three noble trees—a Banyan in the centre, with a Peepul on either side. To the right of the entrance passes off a long avenue of Palmyra palms; to the left runs an avenue of young Asoke and Mahogany trees, while in the middle, and in a line with the gate, runs a broad road which the visitor is recommended to follow. This road, after a little, passes to the left of a large ornamental sheet of water and then through a group of Casuarina trees up the stems of many of which are trained specimens of various species of the climbing palms commonly known as rattans or canes. Emerging from this grove, the road enters the *Palmetum*, a large piece of ground chiefly devoted to the display of members of the noble family of palms.

In the *Palmetum* are some striking avenues of a curious Cuban palm with a columnar white stem. The *Palmetum* is separated from the remainder of the garden by a canal which is crossed by three bridges. Having crossed the canal, the Flower Garden lies to the right. Here are arranged many beds of palms and of succulent and flowering plants. The latter are particularly brilliant during the earlier months of the year. Dotted about in this neighbourhood are the various conservatories devoted to the cultivation of delicate species and of plants not indigenous to India. Notable among these are the two orchid houses, which during the hot season especially present a gorgeous display of bloom; at other seasons the visitor is more struck by the curious forms of stem and leaf displayed by these interesting plants than by their flowers. Near the orchid house is a fine new Conservatory, 200 feet long, for the erection of which funds were granted by the Government of Bengal. Opposite one of the orchid houses stands a monument to the founder of the garden, (General Kyd), and running straight from it to the river entrance ghât is a broad walk flanked on either side by a specimen of that opprobrium of modern English gardening, a ribbon border. Leaving this walk on the left, and passing onward from Kyd's monument, is a road which the visitor should follow. By going along it a few hundred yards, a broad straight road is met with on the right which leads to the great Banyan tree. This wonderful tree is only about a century old. Nevertheless it covers a space of ground 800 feet in circumference. Its trunk girths 51 feet, and from its branches 170 aerial roots descend to the ground. Passing from the Banyan tree in the direction of the river, is all that was spared by the cyclones of 1864 and 1867 of a noble avenue of Mahogany trees which were planted about the end of last century, by Dr. Roxburgh, the second Superintendent of the garden. In the opposite direction from the Mahogany avenue runs another of Debdar trees. On the left of the latter (going from the great Banyan) stands a monument to the celebrated botanist just mentioned, with a Latin epitaph by Bishop Heber, and a little off this road is a space in which a number of plants are scientifically arranged in their natural families.

The gardens abound with plants of interest too numerous for mention here. The visitor in leaving should drive along the avenue which skirts the river, (of which many fine views are obtained) and he should pass out by the Bishop's College gate on the river bank at the south-west corner of the garden. These gardens have a European reputation, and among their Superintendents in past times are to be noted Roxburgh, Wallich, Griffith, Falconer, Thomson, and Anderson, all men of high botanical fame. Formerly containing the finest collection of plants (and especially of trees) in the east, these gardens were desolated by the two cyclones already mentioned, and from the effects of these storms they are only now recovering.

Amongst the benefits conferred on India by these gardens are the introduction of the Tea industry into Assam, and the acclimatization in British Sikkim of the quinine yielding *Cinchonas.* The gardens are open gratuitously every day from sunrise to sunset.

At the north of the garden is BISHOP'S COLLEGE, now the Seebpore Engineering College, beautifully situated, surrounded by green lawns and stately trees. Nearly opposite are the premises of the Messageries Maritimes and the P. & O. Company.

THE PORT AND RIVER.

Turning the elbow of land which projects above Bishop's College, we obtain a noble view of the City and Port of Calcutta, with its splendid buildings and forest of masts.

Just at the point is a handsome residence called *Shalimar*, where Sir John Royds, one of the Judges of the Supreme Court, thirty years ago, enjoyed his learned leisure. Immediately above is the Sumatra sand, an immense sand-bank which has inconveniently narrowed the channel of the river. From this point northward to *Goosery*, including the villages of *Seebpore*, *Ramkistopore*, *Howrah*, and *Sulkeah*, the riverside is the seat of most important industries,—in connection with which the name of WILLIAM JONES should not be forgotten. William Jones, mechanic, arrived in India in 1800. After ten years of struggle, we find him, in 1810, the proprietor of a canvas manufactory at Howrah. In the next year his extraordinary mechanical skill enabled him to start a little paper manufactory, for the manufacture of cartridge paper for Government. Four or five years after, Jones accidentally discovered the existence of coal in the Burdwan district, and with characteristic ardour determined to open the mines. His last public engagement was the building of Bishop's College. That he should have ventured upon so difficult an undertaking, and one so foreign to his previous pursuits, and that he should have succeeded so admirably in the execution of it, is of itself a sufficient demonstration of the lofty enterprise, and genius of the man. His active and useful life was brought to an abrupt close in September 1821, by a fever contracted whilst superintending the building. Like many other men of genius he was incapable of saving a fortune out of the numerous lucrative schemes which he originated. They imparted a great impulse to national improvement, and subsequently proved a source of no little wealth to others, but they brought little benefit to his family, to whom he bequeathed scarcely anything beyond the high esteem and reputation he had so richly earned.

Very extensive premises for the pressing and manufacture of jute have been erected at *Seebpore* and *Ramkistopore.*

Howrah is the Terminus of the East Indian Railway. Here also is the Carriage Manufacturing Department. The premises occupy an extensive frontage. Here and at *Sulkea* are the Docks and ship-building establishments which were finally removed from the Calcutta side about 60 years ago. Some of the docks will accommodate vessels of the largest dimensions. Above Howrah is the village of *Goosery*, where are extensive Cotton Mills, which have been worked for some years with great success.

From this point the right bank of the river presents no objects of interest until we arrive at *Bali*, a village distant by rail 6½ miles from Howrah, and one of the most orthodox and holy places in the neighbourhood. It is said to contain one thousand families of Brahmans. But even here education has worked wonders, and at *Ooterparrah*, an adjoining hamlet, there exists a noble building on the river bank, containing a large Circulating Library, Reading and Lecture-rooms established by Baboo JOYKISSEN MOOKERJEE, a wealthy and philanthrophic zemindar residing there. *Bali* boasts also a Paper Mill, the only one in India, in which jute cuttings are largely utilised. Immediately opposite is *Barnagore*, where are the extensive Mills for the manufacture of gunny bags and pressing jute, in which some 4,000 hands are employed. A little above is *Dukhinsore* with its imposing cluster of temples, erected in 1852.

Passing *Konaghur*, on the right bank, we arrive at *Rishera*, a small village, but rising into importance through the establishment of Jute Mills. Formerly a profitable chintz manufactory existed here, subsequently used as a Silk Mill. More recently Yarn Mills were established, which have now given place to Jute, the great staple of Bengal. Rishera house is a fine old mansion, approached by avenues of trees, some of which are said to have been planted by Mrs. Hastings, when she and Warren Hastings made this villa their temporary residence.

Nearly opposite, on the left bank, is *Agurparah*, with its neat Christian Church and school adjoining. A little above is the great *Rass* temple of Kurdah, and half a mile further a cluster of 24 temples dedicated to Siva. A mile beyond is *Titaghur*, formerly an important Dock-yard. In the year 1801 a ship named the "Countess of Sutherland," 1,445 tons burden, was built here, now the site of several handsome villa residences. Immediately adjoining is

BARRACKPORE PARK

Created by the taste and public spirit of Lord Wellesley, 70 years ago. It is about 250 acres in extent, and is beautifully wooded, and artistically laid out. The present Government House was erected by the Marquis of Hastings. Its situation is admirable, commanding a noble prospect of more than six miles down the river. The principal objects of interest in the Park are Lady Canning's tomb, which occupies a charming spot on the banks of the river, a short distance from the house; and a fine Memorial Hall erected by the Earl of Minto in 1813 "To the memory of the Brave." It contains Tablets to the memory of officers who fell at the conquest of the Isle of France in 1810, and of Java in 1811, and of officers who fell at Maharajpore and Punniar in 1813. There is also in the Park a small Menagerie, and a very pretty Aviary.

In the early part of the year visitors should not omit a visit to the elephant training stables near the race course. The elephants captured in the jungles of Eastern Bengal during the previous cold season generally arrive at Barrackpore towards the end of the year, and remain here a few months to complete their education. 50 to 80 elephants may sometimes be seen. No danger need be feared from them.

Barrackpore is a Military Station, and contains extensive Barracks for the accommodation of European and Native Troops. There is a neat church, and since the opening of the Railway, the town has become very popular as a residence for Europeans. It is reached by the Eastern Bengal Railway in three quarter of an hour from Calcutta, or in a couple of hours by road—a very enjoyable drive.

Three miles from Barrackpore station is *Monirampur*, the site of the Water-works, which supply Calcutta with water. The splendid pumping machinery, the extensive settling tanks, and the filtering beds are well worth inspection. Monirampur house was formerly the residence of Mr. John Prinsep, a great public benefactor, and the father of six sons, all of whom acquired distinction in the Civil and Military Service of Government, at the bar, in the pursuits of trade, and in the walks of science. Mr. Prinsep was for ten years contractor for the Chintz investment of the E. I. Company, and set up an establishment for its manufacture at Monirampur. He also introduced the manufacture of Indigo into Bengal, and supplied the Government with this article for many years. Latterly, he turned his fertile mind to the coinage, set up a Mint at *Pultah* the village immediately to the north of Monirampur, and contracted with Government for the first copper coinage ever struck in Bengal.

A little above *Pultah* are the Government Powder Works at *Ishapore*.

Immediately opposite Barrackpore is

SERAMPORE,

A settlement of the Danes from 1755 to 1845. In 1845 the Danes sold Serampore to the English for twelve lakhs.

The Church with its handsome steeple was built in 1865 at an expense of Rs. 18,500, raised by subscription, of which Rs. 1000 were given by the Marquis of Wellesley. There is also a handsome Roman Catholic chapel, erected by the Barrettos in 1766, and a convent.

Serampore will be ever remembered in connection with the Baptist Mission, founded here in 1799. The founders,—Carey, Ward, and Marshman,—are interred in the Serampore burial-ground. The Chapel in which they preached still exists.

The *Serampore College*, on the banks of the river, is a fine building, erected in 1818, partly from the private funds of the Serampore Missionaries. It has an iron roof, a handsome iron staircase, and a well arranged library, containing some rare works on India.

In front of it stood the house of Dr. Carey; its site is now sixty feet in the river, which has here cut away much of the bank. Dr. Carey's Botanic Garden, established by him in 1800, which contained in its palmy days about 3,000 species of plants, occupied six acres. It is now jungle, and has recently been sold for business purposes. The Serampore Steam Paper Mills, the first set up in India, are now turned into jute screws. There is considerable silk manufacture carried on here, principally in weaving handkerchiefs. There are several large jute mills in the neighbourhood.

Twelve miles further on, by rail, is the French settlement of

CHANDERNAGORE.

It is first mentioned as a French settlement in 1700. But its prosperity dates from the arrival of Mons. Dupleix, the most enlightened and energetic administrator the French have ever had in India. In 1740, while Calcutta was in a state of comparative insignificance, Chandernagore had risen to great opulence and splendour. Dupleix resided in a mansion on the banks of the river, on the site of which stands the present Government House, and there he contemplated the establishment of the French power in this country, and determined himself to lay the foundation of it. In 1793, Chandernagore was captured by the English, and although it was restored twenty-two years after, it has since that time existed as a French establishment without any object, political or commercial. It is now supported by the 300 chests of opium which the French receive annually from the British Government, on condition of their not engaging in the manufacture of that article. Chandernagore is a healthy town and is very pleasantly situated on the river side.

CHINSURAH,

The old Dutch settlement, is within three miles of Chandernagore, and is reached either by rail, or by road, a beautiful drive. It was ceded by the Dutch to the English in

1826, in exchange for the Island of Sumatra. The Fort demolished about fifty years ago, bore the date of 1687. The church was the joint gift of Mr. Sichterman and Mr. Vernet, Governors. Sichterman erected the Steeple in 1744, and Vernet added the Church twenty-four years afterwards, One of the escutcheons in the church refers to a Governor, who died in 1665. The earliest Christian Church in Chinsurah is the Armenian Church, built in 1695. Near this church is the Dutch burial-ground.

A little to the south of the Dutch Church is the "Hoogly College," held in a splendid mansion originally erected by Mons. Perron, a French General, who, fifty years ago, accumulated a large fortune in the Mahratta service. Chinsurah was formerly the depôt for the reception of recruits on their arrival from England, and also for invalids. There are extensive ranges of barracks here, (erected on the site of the old Fort) but they are now disused.

Closely adjoining is the Town and Civil Station of

HOOGHLY.

The Portuguese are stated to have established a factory here in 1540, and to have built a Fort in 1599. In 1625 the Dutch had factories here. In 1631, it was captured by the Mogul army, and became the royal port of Bengal. Previous to the founding of Calcutta, in 1686, Hooghly was the residence of Job Charnock, the English Chief, and his Council.

The *Emambarra* at Hoogly is well worth a visit. It is in charge of a Shaik Moulvi. The mosque is a handsome structure, and there is also a serai for the accommodation of travellers. The entrance is below a lofty and massive clock tower. The chimes are remarkably fine and sonorous in tone. In the Court-yard is a large oblong tank with a fountain in the centre.

The Emambarra was founded with part of a legacy left by Mahomed Muhsin, who died during last century The other part of the legacy is now-a-days used for maintaining several Madrasahs in Bengal, and for scholarships for Mahomedan students.

BANDEL.

A little above the town of Hooghly, there is an old Roman Catholic Chapel and Priory, founded A. D. 1599,—*the oldest Christian Church in Bengal*,* built in the year Queen Elizabeth sanctioned the establishment of the E. I. Company; its steeple can be seen from the Railway station. In consequence of the services rendered by the Portuguese to the King of Goa, Bandel was given to them, and they built a fort opposite it for defence. In Bandel, a century ago, there were a nunnery, a boarding-school, and college of Jesuits, but all have passed away; the church is now only noted for the festival of the Novena, celebrated in November, to which a great number of Roman Catholics resort. When, in 1632, Hooghly was taken by the Moguls, the images and pictures of this church were destroyed by command of the Emperor of Delhi; however, through the influence of one of the priests, who was taken prisoner to Agra, 777 beegahs of rent-free land were granted to Bandel by the Emperor of Delhi. Bandel is famous for its cream cheese.

* The church was burnt during the siege of Hooghly; but the Keystone with the year 1599 in it was used when the church, shortly after 1632, was re-built.

INDEX TO ADVERTISEMENTS OF TRADING FIRMS.

W. Newman & Co. ... ... 3, *Dalhousie Square.*
Thacker, Spink & Co. ... ... 5, *Government Place.*
F. & C. Osler ... ... 12, *Old Court House Street.*
Calcutta Musical Establishment 9, *Chowringhee.*
A. Greenwood & Co. ... ... 3, *Esplanade Row.*
Harold & Co. (Calcutta Musical Depot.) 3, *Dalhousie Square.*
Hamilton & Co. ... ... 8, *Old Court House Street.*
Cooke & Kelvey ... ... 20, *Old Court House Street.*
Jellicoe ... ... 2, *Esplanade Row.*
F. Sebastian ... ... 8, *Dalhousie Square.*
Solomons & Co. ... ... 7, *Government Place.*
C. Lazarus & Co. ... ... 56, *Bentinck Street.*
Dunn & Co. ... ... 46 *and* 47, *Bentinck Street,*
M. Z. Martin & Co. ... ... 4, *Dalhousie Square.*
F. W. Baker & Co. ... ... 9, *Old Court House Street.*
Francis, Ramsay & Co. ... ... 11, *Government Place.*
Ramsay, Wakefield & Co. ... 11, *Government Place.*
Moore & Co. ... ... *Belatee Bungalow.*
C. Lazarus & Co. ... ... 4, *Dalhousie Square.*
T. E. Thomson & Co. ... ... 9, *Esplanade Row.*
Lewis, Stewart & Co. ... ... 5 & 6, *Dalhousie Square, Calcutta.*
Arlington & Co. ... ... 3, *Dalhousie Square.*
The Great Eastern Hotel Co., Limited. ... ... *Calcutta.*
T. O'Neill & Co. ... ... 14, *Government Place.*
W. L. Atkinson & Co. ... ... 5, *Old Court House Street,*
Bathgate & Co. ... ... 16, 17, 18 & 19, *Old Court House Street.*
J. Corfield & Co. ... ... 10, *&* 11, *Esplanade Row.*
G. F. Kellner & Co. ... ... *Calcutta.*
Watson & Summers ... ... 8, *Wellesley Place.*
Cook & Co. ... ... *Dhurrumtollah Street.*
T. F. Brown & Co. ... ... 6, *Dhurrumtollah.*
T. Black & Co. ... ... 55, *Bentinck Street.*